THE FINEST
Nines

The Best Nine-Hole Golf Courses in North America

By Anthony Pioppi
Foreword by Zac Blair

Skyhorse Publishing

Skyhorse Publishing books may be purchased in bulk at special discounts for sales promotion, corporate gifts, fund-raising, or educational purposes. Special editions can also be created to specifications. For details, contact the Special Sales Department, Skyhorse Publishing, 307 West 36th Street, 11th Floor, New York, NY 10018 or info@skyhorsepublishing.com.

Skyhorse® and Skyhorse Publishing® are registered trademarks of Skyhorse Publishing, Inc.®, a Delaware corporation.

Visit our website at www.skyhorsepublishing.com.

10 9 8 7 6 5 4 3 2 1

Library of Congress Cataloging-in-Publication Data is available on file.

Cover design by Tom Lau
Cover photo credit Mark Hess

ISBN: 978-1-5107-2271-2
Ebook ISBN: 978-1-5107-2270-5

Printed in China

Contents

Foreword

By Zac Blair

Without question, the biggest reason I fell in love with the game of golf and for my success in reaching the PGA Tour is that I grew up with a golf course in my backyard.

Mulligans Golf & Games is a nine-hole golf course that my dad designed, owned, and operated. As far back as I can remember, I would spend sun-up 'til sun-down out at Mulligans playing, practicing, or watching my dad beat ball after ball into the back of the driving range.

My dad was a great player in his own right. He was an All-American at Brigham Young University and played on the PGA Tour for a handful of years. He also won basically every State Open west of the Mississippi: Utah, Idaho, Colorado, Wyoming, North and South Dakota—you name it, my dad's name is on the trophy.

Even with all of his experience playing golf at the highest level, my dad always wanted to build a golf course where he could teach someone the correct way to play the game. That someone turned out to be me, and over the years, Mulligans became the place where I learned how to drive, putt, and other fundamentals that have made me the player I am today.

While some people grow up playing regulation 18-hole courses, others, like me, have the opportunity to learn this wonderful game on nine-hole courses that can offer just as much charm and challenge as any 18-hole layout.

These small wonders can be a great place to learn the fundamentals of golf. Because many nine-hole courses are built on smaller pieces of property, they tend to favor skills such as accuracy and shot making—two key fundamentals to becoming a great player.

Even though Mulligans is nine holes, I never believed that it lacked authenticity. I always considered Mulligans to be my very own Augusta National. It was as real as it gets for me, and I could play from dawn to dusk, recreating all the shots I would see the pros make on TV.

So often, nine-hole courses fly under the radar, as people get too caught up with trying to fit in. Nevertheless, these courses are usually much more affordable and accessible than 18-hole courses and are a big reason why so many people learn to love golf.

Some of my very favorite and most influential memories are on nine-hole golf courses. Whether it was learning how to play golf at Mulligans, winning my first Utah Junior Golf Association tournament at Nibley Park Golf Course, or making my way over to Kahuku Golf Course on Hawaii every year before the Sony Open to play with family and friends.

These nine-hole golf courses can be the true hidden gems in the game of golf.

Introduction

Finally!

Nine-hole golf courses are once again getting their due.

With the game in a years-long decline in participation, nine-hole rounds are being pursued as a means by which to reverse the trend.

Research tells us that many modern men, women, and children cannot set aside the four hours or so to play 18 holes. The time needed for nine, however, is acceptable to them.

Also, golfers are once again coming to understand what their forefathers from the last part of the 1800s into the first half of the 1900s knew—that a nine-hole round of golf is perfectly legitimate.

In the post-Second World War days when land was affordable and plentiful and golf was booming, 18 holes became the only acceptable number for the majority of golfers. It was as if the nine-hole game had lost its status. The trend continued into the 2000s, in part because of how the golf press regarded nine-hole layouts. It was rare that a nine-hole facility was featured as a destination or made any best-of lists. In part that changed when the Bandon Dunes golf resort on the coast of Oregon became a smash hit and it was discovered that the first course built by its visionary owner Mike Keiser was The Dunes Club, a nine-hole private club not far from Lake Michigan that is one of the 25 finest nines in North America.

Since then, golfers slowly began to again embrace nine holes.

To that end, the first goal of this book is to recognize and celebrate the finest nines in North America, giving them the validation they have long deserved.

The second objective is to assist in once again legitimizing nines, whether they be public, private, or resort facilities. The third aim is for this book to serve as the impetus for golfers to search out and play the finest nine-hole courses they can find.

How the Courses Were Judged

The ranking criteria for this book focus almost solely on the architecture of the golf courses. They do not take into consideration the clubhouse interior, whether the locker rooms have M&Ms, the practice areas (if there are any), dining choices, or valet parking.

The amount of strategy and shot making needed over the nine holes is chiefly how the courses were evaluated.

Several questions were asked. First, can different classes of golfers negotiate their way from tee to green, or is it a single-lane road that demands the same shot from everyone? On courses that excel architecturally, the crack player can take one route, while the average player has another, and the shorter hitter or less adept still a third.

As an example, on four-par that might mean the boldest player is rewarded for carrying a bunker off the tee with the payoff being a clear shot to the green.

The average player might avoid the bunker but then be challenged to fly a greenside hazard in order to reach the putting surface in regulation. Finally, the player who lacks length can avoid both bunkers, but the cost for doing so is that it will take an extra strike or two of the golf ball to find the putting surface.

The second part of the option yardstick is with regard to the ways in which shots can be played. Courses that allow for the ground game as well as the aerial routes stand above those that don't.

Also, the finest layouts reveal the best players by bringing to the forefront those who have the widest variety of shots in their golf bag. The great courses demand right-to-left and left-to-right ball flights off tees and fairways in order to score. Length, too, is valued, but not on every shot on every hole.

The renowned designs also identify the accomplished putter, chipper, and pitcher with their testing green complexes but do not make recovering from an errant approach shot an arduous task each and every time.

The ultimate putting surface is a "Time Out Green," a putting surface so entertaining that given the opportunity golfers who have finished the hole will take time out of their round to roll a few more putts.

The finest nines were also assessed on the diversity of the par-3s, par-4s, and par-5s.

Course conditions have a minuscule bearing on how a layout was viewed unless the state of the turf was so poor that it was impossible to enjoy the day.

"Perfect" should not be used to describe course conditions. In reality, the word has no meaning in this context.

On some of the great layouts of the world where only Mother Nature provides irrigation, a golf ball stopping in a fairway or on a green does not guarantee an "ideal" result. Yes, it might be sitting delicately atop closely mown turf like a pearl on a jeweler's velvet, but then again it is very possible that the little white orb had found its way into an "imperfect" location, such as a depression, or come to rest on a bare spot or even a flower or weed. At legendary designs such as Machrihanish Golf Club or Fishers Island Club, such "imperfect" lies are routine and accepted not just as normal, but as part of the charm and attraction.

The conditions of a golf course are also inherently weather-related as well as being affected by time of day and the seasons.

For instance, play any layout the day after a three-inch rain and it is unlikely that the greens, fairways, and tees will be rated exemplary, even though they might have been 24 hours prior to the storm.

In areas of North America where *Poa annua,* also known as annual bluegrass, dominates putting surfaces, it is understood that greens might not be as good in the spring as they will be in the fall and that they are at their worst in long light of days' end and best when the sun's rays first illuminate the turf and the mowers have just performed their duties.

The effect that tree plantings, cart paths, and buildings have on the enjoyment of the game was also considered as part of the rating system.

The overall surroundings outside a facility can have some bearing on the experience, but that was given minimal importance. To some, a passing train can be judged as a charming distraction, while others find it an aggravating disturbance.

By the Numbers

In order to make the course descriptions flow and eliminate confusion, the yardage for every layout and every hole is from the back tees.

Twenty-six architects were involved with either the design or redesign of the 25 finest nines. Stanley Thompson, Donald Ross, Jim Urbina, Seth Raynor, Wayne Stiles and John Van Kleek, Gil Hanse, as well as some "unknowns," worked on more than one of the courses found in these pages.

The majority of the layouts are located along the Eastern Seaboard and Mid-Atlantic Region of the United States as well as Eastern Canada. It is from those areas that golf first came to the continent, and in the early days of the game nine-hole designs were common, a trend that continued right up to the Second World War.

By time span, 18 of the layouts are considered Classic Era (built before 1960) and seven are Modern Era. Of those modern layouts, two—Winter Park Golf Course and The Course at Sewanee—were complete renovations of existing Classic layouts. Though the original designs were eradicated, the hole corridors remain.

The oldest facility on the list is Nehoiden Golf Course, which opened in 1900; the newest is renovated Winter Park, which welcomed golfers in 2017.

The US has 20 of the top 25 nines, and Canada has five. The state or province with the most layouts on the list is Massachusetts (five), followed by Connecticut (three). Tennessee, Florida, California, and Ontario each have two. New Brunswick, Manitoba, Alberta, Maryland, New Hampshire, Hawaii, Michigan, Indiana, and New York all have one.

Texas is represented in the chapter on designing a nine-hole layout for the modern golfer.

CHAPTER 1

Whitinsville Golf Club, Whitinsville, Mass.

There is good reason why for so long Whitinsville Golf Club has been considered the finest nine-hole course in the country.

Whitinsville is virtually flawless, a masterwork of a master designer. Architect Donald Ross brought his best to this project, from the first tee to the ninth green.

Over the years there have been musings that part of Whitinsville's greatness belongs to the influence of the construction superintendent on the project, and not Ross. The club, though, possesses the original nine individual detailed hole drawings, each with handwritten notes. They prove Whitinsville was constructed almost exactly to Ross's wishes.

Not surprisingly, the course can be played and enjoyed by golfers of all talent levels, but with every aspect of the game employed in order to score well.

Strategy and options abound. At points, golfers are rewarded for their length off the tee. At other times, putting the driver away and playing for position is the wise move. The long irons as well as the wedges will be called on before the day is done.

Not only do those who trod Whitinsville need a deft putting stroke, but they also need green-reading skills, something that could take many years to acquire since the putting surfaces are brimming with obvious and subtle contours that have developed in the over 90-plus years since the Ross design opened.

The course is made up of one par-5, two par-3s, and six par-4s. Four of the two-shotters are played in a row, but because of their variation in length, elevation, look, and shots required, the span is neither tiresome nor mundane, displaying the genius of Ross.

The two par-3s are worlds apart in their appearance, the skills needed to conquer them, and the shots required to recover if the tee ball ends in unintended locations.

Whitinsville begins with the longest hole on the layout, a 500-yarder, the lone par-5, which doglegs left and at first glance appears to be a gentle hole to which Ross introduced the golfer to the course. It is not.

Perched on a knob, the first green welcomes golfers to Whitinsville with a formidable approach shot that leaves little room for error. (*Anthony Pioppi*)

The fairway is of generous width in the first landing area, but from there to the green the hole forces golfers to make decisions and then adeptly execute.

Between the first and second landing areas and approximately 330 yards from the back tee is a massive swale that runs the width of the fairway. Perhaps as deep as eight feet, it can give pause to the golfer who has muffed or dubbed a drive, acting as a formidable hazard for them that must be carried with a long iron or wood.

Even for the well-played drive, the hole turns into a tester. The green is of the volcano variety, perched atop a plateau with trouble all around. There is a bunker behind, as well as a sharp edge and slope left that can send mishits bounding away. The right side is somewhat more forgiving, with only rough as a penalty. Short right is a large bunker, and short left are a pair of sand hazards cut into a hill, one above the other.

Going for the green in two is an option, but the effort must be flawless in order to guarantee par or better.

For the golfer playing the first as a three-shot hole, there is another worry.

Fifty yards from the center of the green, the fairway abruptly rises to the putting surface, about 30 feet, or at least one club, above the grade. An approach that falls short can easily trickle back down the slope until it reaches level ground.

The closer one gets to the green, the less one can see of the flagstick. That means the more comfortable distance from which to play into the green is farther back, but from there the putting surface appears to be minuscule, the only backdrop being the infinite sky.

The putting surface tilts from back left to front right, so staying below the flagstick is advised.

According to his notes, Ross appears to have found a suitable natural green, giving instruction to "keep the same saucer shape between knolls as now exists."

For probably one of the only times in his career, Ross followed his lengthiest hole on the course with the shortest, and this par-3 is a beauty.

Playing from 140 yards, a golfer will notice that the entirely artificial green site sits 20 feet below the tee. The bunkers, located front left, front right, and right, are carved out of the man-made fill pad.

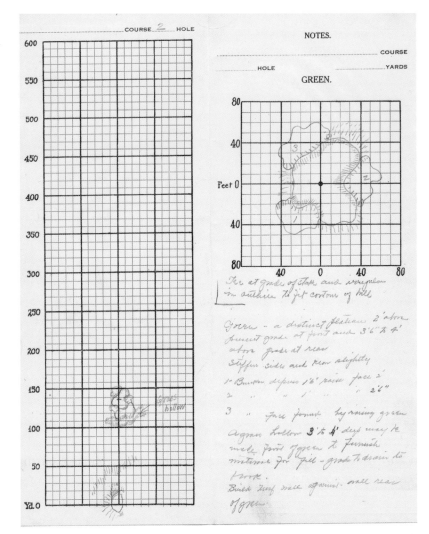

Of the nine hole drawings produced by architect Donald Ross's firm for Whitinsville Golf Club, only the second has a separate sketch for the green, which is described as "a distinct plateau." The instructions call for the front to be two feet above the present grade and the back three and a half to four feet above grade. (*Whitinsville Golf Club*)

Thus, the tee shot is a difficult one to judge even with a short iron in hand. A shot too long avoids sand but finds rough, leaving a tricky recovery to a green that sits between two and four feet above the surrounding land.

From there, golfers cross Fletcher Street and are greeted with a graduate-school lesson in golf course design. Ross displays his brilliance by utilizing a narrow strip of land that can barely accommodate the third and fourth holes with such skill that it would be understood if a first-time Whitinsville golfer went immediately from the fourth green back to the nearby third tee and played the holes again.

The third hole gradually rises from tee to green for all 366 yards, enough so that an extra club is needed for the approach shot. The entire right side of the hole is flanked by out-of-bounds, a fact very much in the players' thoughts as they stand on the tee. To penalize golfers who play too far to the left and away from the OB area, three clusters of fescue-covered mounds await.

Also, for golfers coming into the green from the left side of the fairway, there is a forced carry over bunkers approximately 40 and 70 yards from the middle of the green. They should be no problem if the approach is from the short grass, but from the thick rough or the hummocks, they most certainly come into play.

For the bold golfer who flirted with trouble on the right, the route to the green is open.

The putting surface cants hard left to right, and two greenside bunkers await on the right.

The green is benched into a steep hillside, and any shot that is more than a fraction long most certainly will find deep grass and a nasty lie.

In that same slope Ross carved out the tees for the 350-yard par-4 fourth that plays in the opposite direction of the fifth. It is here that the most substantial alterations have occurred at Whitinsville, probably since the layout opened.

The hole doglegs left, and the knolls that came into play on the previous hole guard the left side here, as well. Playing much shorter because of the elevation, the prime line of play is to cut off the inside of the dogleg, an easier task for the longer hitters. A bunker 280 yards out awaits these hitters' errors.

In 2017, the club wisely removed a large tree on the left side of the hole. It had grown to such stature that many players could not clear it with their drives and were forced to play away from it. For them, the bite-off option was nullified and the hole was one-dimensional.

Consulting architect Gil Hanse suggested taking down the tree and adding mounds farther up in the left rough to penalize off-target long hitters.

Across the way, in the right rough, Hanse recommended building a bunker to inflict hardship on the longer players who miss the fairway.

From any location, the approach shot into the green is a difficult one. The putting surface is guarded left and right by large mounds, portions of which are mowed at green and collar height, an intriguing bit of design flair not found on many Ross layouts. Having to play over the hillocks to the green is a nearly impossible task to complete successfully.

The knobs are the kind of one-off cool, quirky features that makes one wonder if Ross designed them or if they are the diabolical creation of a rogue construction superintendent. The original plans, though, prove they were created in Ross's mind's eye.

He wrote that the mounds should be "three to four feet high with a long grade into the green," and that is exactly what exists.

There is a severe edge to the back of the putting surface, and shots even just a bit long can tumble away. The green is primarily tilted back to front, but there is a lot of other internal movement that if not accounted for will send putts scurrying in unintended and surprising directions.

A barn once sat between the putting surface and the road, but Ross gave instructions for it to be taken down.

Back across Fletcher Street the 421-yard dogleg right fifth looms. It is one of two blind tee shots on the golf course. Here, an angled ridge approximately 100 to 150 yards off the tee obscures the rest of the fairway, but Ross lets golfers know exactly the line to take.

In the left rough are two bunkers. On the right, three bunkers are built into the rise. The gap between the two groups beckons the player. For safety reasons the original teeing ground was moved to the right and away from the second green, so the angle is now slightly off, but the opening Ross designed still serves as a directional indicator for the safe path.

The golfer who takes a bold line and successfully carries the right sand pits will catch the downslope on the far side and receive extra yardage from the kick.

Even with that break, there is still a lot of work to be done. The approach is slightly uphill with two bunkers guarding the left front of the green. Like the previous complex, the back of the fifth is not kind to overzealous shots, and they can easily run 15 yards away before nestling into thick rough.

The front portion is nearly a foot below the rear level. Both sections have more break than what is seen at first glance.

The green sits well back from Mumford River, which can be seen through the trees behind the green. The putting surface, it would seem, should be much closer to

The expansive view from behind Whitinsville's sixth green that extends beyond the fifth green, in the distance, with a portion of the eighth fairway visible on the left. Tree removal in recent years has restored the open feel that architect Donald Ross created. (*Anthony Pioppi*)

the water, but it is not—and for good reason. Apparently, when the course opened in 1925, a dam system along the river was not in place, and the river occasionally flooded the open area. Thankfully, the club has not chosen to mess with Ross's original green and relocate a new one closer to the river.

For the sixth, Ross continues with the same theme—rewarding those golfers who successfully challenge trouble, with the prime angle into the green.

The 385-yarder arcs left to right, and on the inside of the turn are a series of humps adorned in long and thick grass. The axis of the green points to that side of the fairway. For the golfer avoiding the mounds, the fairway is wide and welcoming, but the approach shot is played across a putting surface that cants markedly from back left to front right, away from that line.

There is a special hazard for long-ball hitters who can overdrive the landing zone. About 150 yards from the center of the green, the fairway drops away into rough and then a sliver of a stream.

The land rises again, and the green is situated on the high point. Three bunkers guard the putting surface. There is one short right and one each on the left and right sides.

Seven is the final par-3 and plays from plateau to plateau at 172 yards.

The green is plectrum-shaped with a decided tilt from back to front. According to Ross's notes, a natural "saucer" shape was there, but the back was "stiffened" to improve drainage.

As a result, a recovery shot from beyond the putting surface is a test that even the best short-game players will fail more than they will pass.

Four bunkers await errant tee shots.

Ross gives golfers a bit of a breather on the penultimate hole, a compassionate move on his part, since the show closer is a demanding test.

Eight is a significant dogleg left of only 327 yards. It is a bite-off design that dares golfers to take off as much of the corner as they see fit. The bigger the bite, the shorter the second shot. Longer players who can move the ball right to left have a legitimate chance of driving the green.

In the right rough 230 yards off the tee, a bunker awaits as the only penalty for avoiding the corner.

On the left, three sand hazards, as well as a steep slope that can send errant shots into marshland, inflict pain on poor efforts.

The green has one bunker on the right front corner.

Ross's original design of the hole had an odd setup. He called for the back-most tees to be placed in almost the exact low point of the fairway as the previous hole, meaning golfers on seven would have to play over the heads of their compatriots on the eighth. The existing back/white tee, from which the hole plays 297 yards, is labeled on the Ross plans as the "B" tee. He called for the "A" teeing ground to be constructed 20 yards behind it in the valley and for the "C" to be 10 yards in front of "B" and built up in the small pond.

Playing the eighth from the "B" tee gives the hole a much different feel from the other teeing grounds, with a steep slope obscuring the flat portion of the fairway and the green.

The most heralded hole at Whitinsville is the ninth in what can be described as an utterly stunning creation.

Former PGA Tour player and renowned golf course architect Ben Crenshaw chose it as one of the 18 best Donald Ross holes. Crenshaw reportedly made a special trip to Whitinsville in 1999 when he captained the U.S. Ryder Cup team to a victory at The Country Club in Brookline, Mass.

Ross also thought extremely highly of the ninth. The book *Golf Architecture in America: Its Strategy and Construction*, written by golf architect George Thomas and published in 1927, contains a drawing of the ninth that was contributed by Ross. Though not from the original Ross plan, but an entirely different rendering likely created for the book, a copy of the image hangs in the Whitinsville clubhouse.

The 416-yard ninth is designed to be played across three plateaus—tee, fairway, and green. The hole bends to the right, so not surprisingly, trouble is on that side, and oh what unpleasantness is to be found. The right edge of the hole falls hard approximately 20 feet to a narrow strip of rough that will most likely not thwart errant shots from ending in a marshy cove of Linwood Pond.

However, the distance the modern golf ball flies can eradicate the original Ross strategy, while creating a new conundrum. A drive that travels more than 230 yards will likely catch a slope that will send golf balls tumbling to a valley that, while providing a level lie, offers no view of the green or flagstick. So the question posed to golfers becomes, does one lay up off the tee and see the green on the approach, or does one play a shorter iron into an unseen target?

Three bunkers defend the severely tilted putting surface. Approximately 45 yards from the center of the green in the left rough sits one hazard that in all likelihood must be played over for those approaching from the left rough. Sand also flanks the left and right sides of the carpet.

According to the Ross plan, the land required little work to create the desired putting surface on the world-class finisher. Instructions on the Ross drawing direct that the front of the green be lowered one foot, but "otherwise natural."

BEYOND THE GREEN

Northbridge contains a portion of the John H. Chafee Blackstone River Valley National Heritage Corridor, a National Park dedicated to the birthplace of the American Industrial Revolution. Visitors can also stroll or paddle along the Blackstone River and visit historic sites.

CHAPTER 2

Sweetens Cove Golf Club, South Pittsburg, Tenn.

Without a doubt, Sweetens Cove Golf Club is the finest 9-hole golf course built in the Modern Era of golf course architecture (post-1959), and the second best 9-hole course in North America.

Rob Collins was the chief architect; he was formerly on Gary Player's design team. Tad King was the shaper. He has worked for nearly every big-name architect and pushed dirt on layouts in places like the country of Jordan.

Located in South Pittsburg, Tenn., Sweetens abounds in enjoyment for all golfers. Visually, from the first tee on, it stops players in their tracks. Situated in the Central Tennessee Valley on the Alabama border, the course is surrounded by the heavily wooded Cumberland Plateau, including Monteagle Mountain.

Gnarly-edged sandy waste areas and bunkers populate the course. They are aesthetically pleasing, fitting perfectly into the surroundings, and yet at the same time are often visually intimidating.

The key with hazards, though, is almost all of them can be avoided, since there is plenty of room to tack around them, thanks to mammoth fairways.

On all nine of the holes, approach shots can be run onto the putting surface. Sometimes, however, flying the ball to the green is the play with the greatest reward.

There are two defining characteristics of Sweetens. First is the multiple ways in which one can play the holes. Second are the huge greens that at times surge and fall like storm-churned ocean waves. Yet for each swell, some rising as much as six feet above the surrounding grade, there are calm pools where flagsticks and cups are placed.

Although putting from one level to the other can be dismaying at first, once the basic skill necessary is attained, rolling the rock is a downright blast.

Ask a modern golf course architect who has had the most influence on them, and you'll hear the familiar names of Charles Blair Macdonald, Seth Raynor, Alister Mackenzie, Donald Ross, A.W. Tillinghast, or Pete Dye.

Ask Collins who inspired him when laying out Sweetens Cove, and the answer will be Salvador Dalí—yes, the surrealist artist—and his paintings such as *The Persistence of Memory,* where clock faces drip off a tree branch, a table, and a deceased duck.

The 7th green at Sweetens Cove is typical of the design style of architect Rob Collins, who cites the work of surrealist painter Salvador Dalí as an influence. (*Rob Collins*)

Much like Dalí's timepieces, Collins's green surfaces trickle over the edges of fill pads as if they were perpetually oozing their way toward fairways and approaches.

Ironically, Sweetens occupies the former site of Sequatchie Valley Country Club. Calling what was there a rudimentary design would be gracious. The nine holes sat on a mahjong board-flat piece of ground that the talented King and his machines transformed. Every mound and hollow is manufactured but appear natural as if they were there as long as the surrounding hills.

Overall, the layout is guided by the tenets of Macdonald and Mackenzie, who touted extremely wide fairways with numerous paths to get from tee to green and a dearth of rough in which golf balls could be lost, slowing down play and increasing frustration. Golf is meant to be fun, after all.

That style is evident on the first hole, a par-5, where golfers who know the course look for the flagstick 560 yards away before teeing off. The side of the green on which the hole is located determines the best path from which to play, as a large bunker in the middle of the approach obscures portions of the putting surface, depending on where one stands in the fairway.

The task of getting to the preferred spot is not a simple one, as bunkers left and right await poor shots. There is plenty of room to miss, though; the landing areas for the tee shot and second shot are 70 yards wide.

The green features a high-backed Punchbowl design left and a more sedate lower right tier—overall, a rather tranquil putting surface compared to what is in store.

On the second hole the player gets a simple lesson in how just one properly placed bunker can create strategy and confuse the thought process.

The hazard is located smack in the center of the fairway landing area on the 375-yard straightaway hole that has out-of-bounds abutting the entire left side and a nasty unkempt area down the right.

The options presented to the golfer are simple when it comes to the bunker—stay short, play over, or avoid it to the left or the right, where there is 30 yards of short grass on either side. The wind, firmness of the turf, and, most important, resolve of the golfer are all factors in determining the correct approach.

The green has not a bunker guarding it and the only real penalty for a missed approach is well right, but the entire surface is seemingly one swale after another, making holing a putt of any length a formidable undertaking.

The third hole, from start to finish, is a puzzle that has many correct answers, none of which is easy to attain. The par-5 can be reached with two superior blows, but it is no simple task, as the hole is rife with penalties.

Off the tee there is considerable trouble—to the right in the form of a long sandy waste area and to the left, where out-of-bounds runs the length of the hole. The prudent play just might be to leave the driver in the bag and lay up.

Like hole no. 1, though, the second shot is determined by the flag location on the ultrawide plateau green. Here, a 60-foot-tall pine tree in front of the left third of the putting surface is the hazard that demands to be avoided.

Other than playing around the tree, the only other option is to run a shot underneath the branches to the three-tiered putting surface whose highest shelf is six feet above the approach.

A sand waste area is long and to the left of the green, while the rest of the minimesa is surrounded by fairway.

Birdies are plentiful here, but so are bogies or worse—a testament to the successful risk-reward element of the design.

Up next is the first par-3 at Sweetens, the memorable fourth hole, a joy to encounter each and every time.

The hole stretches from 80 yards to 200 yards and features a colossal 20,000-square-foot meandering green—roughly the size of Liechtenstein—that is 85 yards long. It has more shelves than a Super Kmart and more twists and turns than a Knut Hamsun plot.

The fourth is called "King," the only hole at Sweetens with a moniker, named after the late King Oehmig. It was Oehmig who suggested a hole have a green patterned on the famous Himalayas green at the iconic Prestwick Golf Club in Scotland. The fourth was also influenced by the 10th hole at Friar's Head golf course on Long Island, N.Y., a Ben Crenshaw-Bill Coore design.

Oehmig, a Chattanooga native, was, in addition to being an Episcopal Reverend, a talented golfer and longtime coach of the Baylor School's girls' and boys' golf teams.

He was also a member of the Royal and Ancient Golf Club of Scotland. Oehmig played a significant role in the King-Collins duo getting the Sweetens job. Golf was such a significant part of Oehmig's life that it was prominently mentioned in his obituary:

"King's knowledge and passion for course design played an instrumental role in the development of several golf courses, including the redesign of Lookout Mountain Golf Club and The Course at Sewanee (the 13th-ranked nine-hole course in North America), and the layout of Black Creek Club and Sweetens Cove Golf Course."

At the fourth hole, the lowest portion of the green is the front, with the rest of the putting surface higher.

The green is so large and twisty that it is possible to be on the putting surface but have no way to get to the hole with one putt. It is also feasible to have the golf ball tumble off the green and come to rest far enough away from the cup that the next shot will be with a lofted club and not a blade.

The immense area can also produce epic results, such as 150-foot putts that break four times and come to rest within tap-in distance of the hole, the kind of thrilling experiences that are talked about for years.

The fifth hole is the first of two short par-4s at Sweetens. Both display Collins's grasp of the risk-reward strategy and the fun inherent in it. Seemingly easy to conquer, neither proves to be unless every shot from start to finish is well planned and executed.

At 293 yards from the back tees, the fifth is drivable, but sand guards the entire right side, including a bunker that creeps in on the green.

There is ample room to avoid that trouble; the fairway is 85 yards wide at one point. The only trouble to the left side is a lone tree at the fairway's edge about 170 yards out. But playing that way and away from the optimum line can mean having to carry a left greenside sand pit on the approach shot. This sand pit has the nasty characteristics—small and deep—of the famed Road Hole Bunker on the 17th hole of the Old Course in St. Andrews, Scotland.

From the centerline, the middle of the putting surface is backstopped by a gradual rise that with its Punchbowl characteristic can bring a long shot back to the green.

Left and right of that, though, the green complex drops off severely; a misplay on the approach shot can mean a golf ball that, once it falls off an edge, can easily run 25 yards away.

The shortest par-4 at Sweetens is followed by the longest par-4, the sixth hole, which plays 456 yards.

Play down the left side off the tee, where a pond stands sentinel, and that results in the best angle into the green, albeit with a carry over water on the approach. Play away from the problem, and from that angle the approach shot is longer and the putting surface is narrower and less receptive.

Here, though, is where Collins and King added an almost disguised defense.

Unlike the front level, the approach from the right rises sharply with the carpet, guarded left by water and in back by water and sand.

A pitch, putt, or chip from just off the green is a formidable challenge as the rise needs to be scaled, but an overzealous shot can easily roll off the green and into considerable trouble.

At hole no. 7, golfers again find themselves faced with a risk-reward, short par-4. This is another hole that provides golfers multiple ways to go from tee to green, each avenue with its own set of problems. Choices must be made and indecisions avoided.

The seventh plays about 313 yards and ends at a plateau green.

The right side of the fairway is dotted with pines. It is the right that is the optimal route to play if going for the green in one. As far as the left option, some 235 yards away is a sizeable sand waste area that just waits to ensnare the off-line drive. For those electing to lay up, there is plenty of room short of the trouble, leaving an approach shot of somewhere in the neighborhood of 110 yards.

The putting surface is tame in the sense that there are no radical slopes or swales, but even so it has a tendency to reject golf balls, as if it is somehow opposed to them, whether they arrived there on the ground or in the air, via driver, wedge, or any club in between.

The final two-shotter, the eighth hole, is 387 yards, and here the putting surface is the star. It has attributes of the Biarritz-style green popularized by Macdonald-Raynor-Banks as well as the 16th hole on the legendary West Links in North Berwick, Scotland.

A deep swale running perpendicular to the line of play bisects the long putting surface. The most famous version is the ninth hole on The Course at Yale.

Collins and King rotated their elevated green complex approximately 45 degrees to the left, meaning the line of play into the hole is likely to be across the narrow putting surface and not with it. The North Berwick green is also rotated left to the line of play at nearly the same angle.

At Sweetens, two smallish bunkers on the left guard the fairway, while to the right a few trees and, in a nice design touch, a bunker are also in play. Both help reel in errant shots.

As with the opening hole, the decision on the way to play the eighth depends on the flagstick location. The green is 12,000 square feet, the second largest on the course.

A view of Sweetens Cove from behind the wild ninth green, which has design attributes of two famous template holes—the Short and Redan. (*Rob Collins*).

Favoring the right side with the tee ball works at times, as does challenging the left bunker on other occasions.

On the approach shot, precision is absolutely necessary because of the dominating swale that has most likely taken up a permanent place in the golfing memory of anyone who has encountered it.

Rolling a golf ball through the hollow, which is wide enough to easily accommodate hole locations, is not an easy undertaking especially if two-putting is the goal. Figuring the correct down-then-up speeds is not an innate ability for most people who aren't employed by the physics department at MIT.

Sweetens concludes with a memorable short par-3, a potential roller coaster ride on a hole that is just 140 yards at its longest.

The design combines two of the most famous par-3 styles in the world, the Redan and the Short.

The hole fits the Short template style in that it is a tee shot of not much length, to an ample putting surface surrounded by trouble.

The Redan feature is on the right third of the green, where a slope that looks like a high-banked NASCAR turn covered in low-mown turf allows players to roll the ball from the lower right level to the middle level, or in some cases, all the way to the lower left portion. It is a Time Out Green that beckons players to remain there after the round in order to experience myriad thrilling putts the complex presents.

The ninth green just might have some magic built into it as well, as it was the location of two astounding feats within a matter of a few hours.

In 2016, during a girls' high school golf tournament, two players aced the ninth hole on consecutive swings, a 17-million-to-1 happening. Then, during the same tournament, another golfer, playing in the final group of her team's match, gave her school a one-shot victory with the third ace of the day.

There have been 15 aces on the ninth hole since the course opened in October 2015. There are sure to be many more.

Beyond the Green

South Pittsburg is a town of roughly 3,000 inhabitants, but if you are there on the right weekend in the spring, check out the National Cornbread Festival.

South Pittsburg is also the home to Lodge Cast Iron, one of the largest manufacturers of cast iron cookware in the country. Lodge is owned and managed by two great-grandsons of the founder, Joseph Lodge. The company's foundry in South Pittsburg, in operation since the business opened, produces the bulk of the cast iron.

For those who desire more nine time, Sewanee Golf Course, the 13th-ranked 9-hole course in North America, is 30 miles away.

Then there is Chattanooga, a flourishing city 20 miles from Sweetens, with a vibrant downtown including an actual distillery on Main Street—the Chattanooga Whiskey Co.—as well as a thriving restaurant, bar, and live music scene and a world-class aquarium. Is a beer and a burger what you need? Seek out the Tremont Tavern. The Durty Gomez burger is recommended.

CHAPTER 3

Culver Academies Golf Course, Culver, Ind.

For decades the golf course at Culver Academies existed as if it were a painting hanging on the wall of a long-abandoned home, covered in soot, dust, and grime. If one looked intently enough, the forms and images could be discerned, but the true artistry was hidden by years of neglect.

Prior to restoration, every original bunker was overgrown with grass, putting greens had shrunk a third or more of their intended sizes, and trees encroached on fairways that had decreased significantly in width.

Students played on the course more as a lark rather than an actual golfing endeavor.

Then in 2013 it was decided that the course that had opened in 1924 should be returned as close as possible to its original greatness.

The result of the work by architect Bobby Weed and his senior design associate, Chris Monti, is stunning.

Culver was originally laid out by the midwestern architecture team of William Langford and Theodore Moreau, considered by many to be the most underrated designers of the period from around 1910 to the start of the Second World War, known as the Golden Age of Architecture. Their most famous work is The Golf Courses of Lawsonia Links course in Green Lake, Wisconsin.

The Culver layout brims with angles and strategy, as well as the trademark Langford-Moreau large greens that possess bold interior contouring. There are also the severe outside edges of the green fill pads that dispatch poor shots into bunkers, rough, or worse, a style that conjures up the work of Charles Blair Macdonald, Seth Raynor, and Charles Banks. What Langford and Moreau created at Culver might be the finest set of green complexes on any nine-hole golf course in North America.

Every putting surface is open in front, so the option of running shots onto the green is available. Since the Culver layout is now kept in firm condition, the choice of playing the ball on the ground is there and often a wise one.

The nine holes actually comprise part of a larger project that was never completed. In the early 1920s Culver Academies, then known as Culver Military Academy, located

The third hole at Culver ends at a fun bold green surrounded by large, aesthetically pleasing bunkers ready to penalize poor shots. (*Lew Kopp*)

roughly 40 miles south of South Bend, Ind., had the audacious idea to construct 27 holes, three nines, that began and ended at one location. Langford and Moreau drew up plans, but for reasons that have been lost to history, only nine were built. The holes they constructed were taken from the first and second nines of the planned 27. They were originally holes 10-11, 8-9, 1-2, 16-18. As a result, golfers of today who play do so over the two starting and two finishing holes of what would have been first nine as well as the two starting and three finishing holes of the second nine.

The existing routing has three par-5s, par-4s, and par-3s. From the back, Culver plays 3,328 yards.

The layout begins with arguably the weakest hole, a confounding par-5 that violates a basic rule of architecture, yet in the end still somehow works.

The uphill tee shot is over a gorge, populated by all sorts of unfriendly plant life like dense bushes and thickets, to a large flat area guarded on the left by a bunker in the rough. Into the wind and on a cold day, reaching the fairway can be a task.

From here it gets a little kooky.

The hole banks hard to the left but the land falls severely to the right, the exact opposite of how it should work. Think of it as a racetrack—when turning left, the track banks from right to left.

The longer and bolder golfer can fire a shot over a massive, steep-walled bunker in the left rough. Carrying it by just 10 yards or so can result in the ball running a hundred yards and possibly onto the green. Miss left, however, and the bunkers of the third green come into play.

The real problem on the first hole, though, is for the player who lays up on the second shot. Because of the severity of the canted fairway, a shot that lands anywhere on the slope will not stop until it finds the right rough, or a bunker that sits 90 yards from the center of the green. Even well-struck efforts that find the fairway just inside the left rough line don't come to a halt until the long grass or sand on the right takes hold.

The green is large and wonderful, an accurate introduction to what lies ahead on the other eight holes.

The second hole is a testing uphill, right-to-left par-3 with four bunkers that guard a green, which is open in front and runs away from the line of play. It is possibly a

Langford-Moreau version of a Redan green, but milder than ones designed by Raynor or A.W. Tillinghast.

The third hole, another 1-shotter, is among the most exquisite par-3s of any hole on any course. It plays 174 yards on the ground—but shorter in reality since the hole descends the ridge that the second one ascended.

Although the back-to-back par-3s are almost identical in length, they almost always play at least a two-club difference because of elevation alone and can easily be as much as four clubs apart with a slight wind.

Five bunkers protect the two-tier putting surface that is shaped like a light bulb with the wider portion at the front.

The bunker on the right snuggles up to the green, while the ones on the left are back and well below the putting surface. A shot that barely misses the green will almost always find sand.

In an interesting twist to the norm, instead of the right of the green being the lowest portion and the left the highest, Langford and Moreau flipped it—the right is the highest with a nearly two-foot drop off to the left section.

For the golfer, the gutsy move to get near a back left pin might be to fly it there, but a well-played shot with a right-to-left ball flight that lands on the upper shelf will find its way to the lower portion, much to the enjoyment of all on the tee who watch the drama unfold.

For the next hole, golfers make a 180-degree turn as it is again up the ridge, this time in the form of a tantalizing bite-off dogleg par-4.

That area that needs to be bitten can accurately be described as golfing hell or the land of no return, part of the same netherworld that players crossed with the drive off the first hole. A golf ball that lands there is irretrievable.

There is one long left bunker short of the green that is in play for the monster hitters. There is also one greenside bunker on the right. The defense for the back of the green is a sharp vertical edge. Balls that run through the putting surface can find the first tee.

The practice range is to the right of the fourth hole, and that area has an interesting history. At one point that expanse was a runway for the school's aviation program, which has long been disbanded.

The fourth hole at Culver has a risk-rewards tee shot that tempts golfers to bite off the corner with a shorter second shot as the reward. Missing to the left, though, is disastrous. (*Anthony Pioppi*)

The walk from the fourth green to the fifth tee brings players past the ninth green and the new golf house, to the second loop of holes and the second par-5 of the round. It is the best of the three, as well, measuring 491 yards.

A slight dogleg left, this hole serves as a reward to the long hitters. The tee shot is uphill until about 260 yards, when the fairway falls away from the line of play. A golf ball catching the slope can run on upwards of 40 yards, and from there the green can be reached in two strokes.

On this hole, though, the average player might feel constrained for the first time in the round. There is a forest off the right side of the hole and newly planted trees on the left that are there to protect buildings of the Culver Summer School and Camps, which are set well back from the hole corridor.

In a quirk of Culver, the fifth hole is closed for six weeks in the summer when camp is in session. During that time golfers walk from the fourth green to the practice range tee and play a 190-yard par-3 to a practice green, then head over to the actual sixth tee.

Other than the trees, the second landing area is unguarded, although the undulating land rarely yields a level lie.

The fifth ends at a genuine Time Out Green that just might be the best on the course. It is a world-class design that is 35 yards wide and 28 yards deep, rising from front left to back right and inundated with humps and pockets.

As a result of the entertaining design, some extra putts are expected.

Behind the putting surface is a building that acts as a storm shelter and summer camp classroom. Culver alumnus Roger Penske, who also contributed to the restoration of the golf course and is best known as the owner of Team Penske auto racing, donated it.

The sixth hole, at 407 yards, is a dogleg right. The bend is early in the hole and, along with a bunker and trees on the inside of the dogleg, can create an uncomfortable feeling for those looking to take the optimal line down the right. The left, in contrast, is wide open, but Langford and Moreau have plenty in store for the golfer playing in that direction.

First, there is a massive bunker half in the rough and half in the fairway approximately 300 yards out. It can still have plenty of impact for those who can't reach it. The sand is flashed so high that it blocks the view of the green from the far left fairway or the left rough.

Get too far left on the approach shot to the green, and another massive sand hazard waits. Those who land there can be left with a bunker shot of up to 40 yards.

The architects threw an amusing wrinkle into the green. At the right front corner is a tricky mound that takes skill to negotiate when putting or chipping over. It is the only such feature on a Culver green. The remaining portion of the sixth's putting surface is packed with movement.

Although not the longest of the par-4s, the seventh is an extremely difficult hole at 419 yards.

Opposite of the sixth, this hole bends left. Large bunkers on the inside of the turn only allow golfers to see a small portion of the fairway. The illusion is the hazards seem farther off the tee than they really are. Add to that the fact that the tree line, which could stand a significant trimming, seems to be hanging over the fairway, so the natural tendency is to play away to the open right side. Do that, and it makes the uphill approach shot that much longer, easily playing over 200 yards from there.

There is a penal bunker short and left of the putting surface and one greenside right.

The green is the subtlest on the course, not surprising considering the high degree of difficulty on the approach. It tilts back to front with the sides higher than the middle, resulting in a shallow concave design.

The final par-3 is the eighth hole, which measures 150 yards. The green leans from back to front and is shaped like a water droplet, with the narrower end closest to the tee. A thin, long strip bunker guards either side.

From the tee it seems like a relatively easy hole but does not play that way. Maybe the green is not as far below as it seems, maybe the sand is more intimidating than first thought, or the severe drop-off that awaits the overly forceful shot weighs more on the mind than realized.

Of course, Langford and Moreau put plenty of swales and depressions into the putting surface.

Culver ends in much the same way it started, with a quirky par-5. The ninth, at 481 yards, appears straightforward from the tee; it is anything but that.

The slightly uphill tee shot is visually intimidating, the result of two bunkers cut into the rough before the fairway begins, which confounds the players' depth perception.

Here, length is a tremendous advantage. A tee shot that covers the first 240 yards will leave 220 yards or so into the green, but a tee ball that flies a bit farther can catch a steep downslope and easily get 50 more yards of roll, coming to rest in a large, deep saddle.

The catch is that from there the green is completely blind and the golfer is left staring at a sharply rising wall of fairway.

The preferred line off the tee for golfers who cannot drive it down the hill is to the right. On the next shot two bunkers on the right often must be flown. The good news is that beyond them the fairway runs down toward the green.

Golfers who play out to the left are met with a massive intimidating bunker that Langford and Moreau placed so that it must be carried by those looking for the optimum line on the second shot. The back edge of the hazard is 130 yards from the center of the green, but because of the steep topography that tilts to the right and the superb firmness of the golf course, shots that just clear the menacing bunker will run on seemingly forever, possibly making their way to the putting surface.

The lone greenside bunker is a large horseshoe affair on the right that is not fun to play out of, especially if the flag is on that portion of the green, which runs hard away to the left.

"The sign of a great nine-hole course is one that can be played twice in a row from the same tees and still be enjoyable," architect Monti said.

According to those criteria and others, Culver easily meets the standards.

See for yourself. The distance from the ninth green to the first tee is all of 45 yards. It is an easy walk and one that begs to be made.

Beyond the Green

Culver is a happening place in the summer, thanks to Lake Maxinkuckee.

For Michael Vessely, the superintendent of the Culver Academies course, there is really only one answer regarding what to do once golf is done:

"I think the most interesting thing in Culver is the Academy itself. I tell people that the golf course is a great story, but if you tie it in with the story and history of the Academy, it becomes more special. There is the Steinbrenner Recreation Center (named after alum George Steinbrenner); Huffington Library named after Michael Huffington (who, along with his former wife Arianna, founded the *Huffington Post*); and Henderson Ice Arena, named after Jim Henderson's family (former CEO of Cummings Engines). There is one of the largest indoor equestrian arenas in the world, and the school's Black Horse Troop has marched in almost every presidential inauguration since the start of the 1900s."

CHAPTER 4

The Dunes Club, New Buffalo, Mich.

W hen The Dunes Club opened in 1990, not far from the shore of Lake Michigan, there was barely a ripple in the golf course architecture world even though what Dick Nugent designed was easily the best nine-hole layout built in the Modern Era.

Back then, though, the owner of the course had not yet changed the world of golf. That would not occur until 1999, the year that Mike Keiser's Bandon Dunes Golf Resort on the southern coast of Oregon with the David McLay Kidd design opened.

Two years later Pacific Dunes, a Tom Doak layout, was added, and then followed Bill Coore and Ben Crenshaw's Pacific Trails in 2005. The final piece (for now) came in 2010 with Old Macdonald, a Doak-Jim Urbina collaboration that pays homage to Charles Blair Macdonald.

As more eyes turned toward Bandon, The Dunes Club was finally recognized and given its due as one of the finest nine-hole golf courses in North America.

The course remained relatively unchanged until 2016 when Urbina, now on his own, made substantial modifications to the layout, especially on and around the greens.

To give an idea of what he was looking for, Keiser had taken Nugent to see his favorite golf course, Pine Valley Golf Club, carved out of the pine barrens of Southern New Jersey, and considered by many not only to be the best golf course in the United States, but also in the world. PV is about sand in the form of waste areas and large greenside bunkers that exact heavy tolls on errant shots. Also set amidst pines, the

Dunes Club has the feel of PV but on a smaller scale, lacking the breadth and width of its inspiration.

The Dunes is a private club with fewer than 100 members. There is no driving range, and the "clubhouse" is smaller than a lot of halfway houses at exclusive facilities. There are also no tee markers. It is a layout designed to be tested in match play with the winner of the previous hole selecting where on the next teeing ground the hole will commence. The differences from one location to another can be 95 yards and at substantially different angles, in the case of one par-3.

Urbina said his focus for the renovation was to add some variety to the greens, as four of the originals had two tiers with the back always the higher one. He also reworked fill pads and green surrounds, removing severe features so the ground game became more of an option. Fairway and approach mowing lines were altered, and Urbina called for the removal of trees and undergrowth to increase sunlight and airflow throughout the nine holes, which lead to healthier turf and firmer conditions.

Urbina performed alterations on nearly every one of the holes, but he lauds much of the Dick Nugent original design, especially the greens on the second and fourth holes.

"Two and four are just good, good on the ground," Urbina said. "You could base 18 greens on those two holes."

Keiser's son Michael, a member at The Dunes Club, said the goal of the renovation was to improve the experience at all the holes, using Urbina's favorites as the benchmark.

For golfers who have not been to The Dunes Club since the reworking, it will be obvious from the first hole, a 415-yard par-4, that changes have taken place.

The green was lowered by two feet, and the putting surface was reworked to give it more movement and more areas in which a flag can be planted. A back left bunker was added and mounding was reshaped.

Very little was done to the second hole, a downhill par-3 that plays 200 yards from the back and 130 from the front, the tee shot over a sandy expanse. Urbina is effusive in his praise of the bilevel putting surface.

"I wouldn't touch that for anything."

Vegetation was choking sections of the third hole, a par-5 of 534 yards, so Urbina opened up the tee shot to give golfers a better aiming point and help dry out the fairway. As a result, the ball rolls much better, and that can make players think more about which club to hit off the tee on the slight dogleg right.

It is on this hole that Nugent created his version of the great hazard, which appears on the seventh at Pine Valley, a design feature suggested by the architect A.W. Tillinghast on many layouts, including Bethpage Black and Newport (R.I.) Country Club.

The large sand area short and left of the green, which dominates a player's eye on the approach, now shows better with the tree removal. The portion to the left of the putting surface was enlarged. The left portion of the green was improved, as well.

On the 422-yard fourth hole, which bows slightly to the left, tree and brush removal was also completed.

The reworked eighth green of The Dunes Club. Architect Jim Urbina accentuated the Punchbowl aspects of the original putting surface. (*Margo James*)

Urbina stretched the fairway there as well, so it is now the widest on the course. He also reworked a knob to the left of the putting surface, creating the option to run the ball onto the green.

"It's really fun to play," Urbina said.

A sandy area on the left side of the fairway up near the green was expanded to make it more of a factor.

For many players, the 412-yard fifth is a layup hole. While the nearest point of the pond that runs the width of the fairway is 300 yards away, the combination of a downhill tee shot, a tailwind, and firm turf can make it reachable.

It is the elevated green complex, which requires at least an extra half club to reach, that defends the hole.

"It reminds me of a [Perry] Maxwell green," Urbina said.

Maxwell, a prominent architect during the Golden Age of design, reworked Augusta National, including the existing greens, and designed a number of the phenomenal courses including the first nine at Prairie Dunes Country Club in Hutchinson, Kansas, where his son Press later added nine more.

In front of the putting surface is a prominent knob that repels shots in all directions, including back down the severe slope. Urbina left the feature as he found it.

"It's crucial to the green. We would never touch it," he said.

What he did do was expand and rework the back of the green, adding a rise so that players can now send their shots over or around the front mound and the golf ball will come back to the putting surface where he added contouring.

Nowhere at The Dunes Club was more work done than on the sixth hole, which plays 185 yards from the back.

The most obvious of the alterations was the addition of the Blueberry Tee.

For the original teeing grounds, players took a left off the back of the fifth green, walking nearly a hundred yards. Now, there is the option to tread straight off the green and go a short distance to the new tees that play 105 yards from the front and 115 yards from the back.

In addition, the current green bears little resemblance to the two-tiered one that was there before. There is now only one level, and the putting surface on the right was extended.

The most significant change architect Jim Urbina made at The Dunes Club is the addition of the Blueberry Tee on the par-3 sixth hole that can play over 200 yards. From the new tee, the middle of the putting surface is no more than 115 yards away. (*Margo James*)

"There is much more movement and interesting pin locations," Urbina said.

The approach also underwent substantial changes.

At seven, significant modifications were made to the green on the hole that can play up to 385 yards. The putting surface originally leaned from back to front but now slopes left to right and, according to Urbina, "is more conducive to the run-on shot."

He also increased the size of the green by extending the back right section.

Urbina is proud of what he calls a "uni-tee," constructed in a location that plays shorter than the existing back tees. The complex has a multitude of options and gives golfers the choice of teeing off high or low and left or right.

Down the left side of the hole corridor, trees were thinned and a bunker was added as well, to provide a challenge to golfers taking that route to the green.

Hole number eight might shock those players who experience it for the first time, as the green size was doubled. Nugent's design was a Punchbowl, and Urbina made it more prominent.

"My dad loves Punchbowls," Michael Keiser said.

Urbina also removed trees behind the putting surface to give it more of an open feel and to make the bowl characteristic more prominent. The green was enlarged from front right to back left, and there is a profusion of movement within the bowl. As they should, the walls will hold in approach shots that might have a little too much on them, except for the back left corner, which is devoid of forgiveness.

The look and playability of the approach was modified, too, so shots can make their way onto the green in a variety of ways.

"It lets you be creative," Michael Keiser said.

For the final hole, Urbina performed only a modicum of work, reshaping the front left greenside bunker and softening the approach. He also adjusted the fairway lines and opened an area behind the putting surface. Golfers can now enjoy their one and only view of Lake Michigan from the course.

BEYOND THE GREEN

Suffice it to say there is something to do every weekend and almost every day in and around New Buffalo. For instance, there is the St. Mary of the Lake Family Festival, Three Oaks Music in the Park, Three Oaks Theater Festival, NBYC Corn and Sausage Roast, Ship & Shore Festival, Michigan's Longest Garage Sale, Kee-Boon-Mein-Kaa Pow Wow (celebrating the huckleberry harvest), St. Paraskevi Greek Festival, and the New Buffalo Harvest and Wine Fest.

Beer Church Brewing Co. offers beer and pizza.

CHAPTER 5

Fundy National Park Golf Course, Alma, NB, Canada

Stanley Thompson holds the undisputed title of greatest Canadian golf course architect, and so it is fitting that one of his creations is Canada's finest nine. The Fundy National Park Golf Course, located in New Brunswick, is part of a national park that also includes the Bay of Fundy, which has the highest tides in the world, rising and falling more than fifty feet in some locations on a normal day.

The golf course opened in 1948, making it one of Thompson's final works. The common narrative is that Thompson designed an 18-hole layout for Fundy, like he had for his other national parks including Banff and Cape Breton Highlands, but that the second nine was never built and what is there now was never intended to stand alone.

Thompson's plans, however, appear to tell a different story. Holes one through six are marked appropriately, but then there is a change. Holes seven through nine on what is the existing course are numbered 7/16, 8/17, and 9/18. The remaining holes, the ones never built, number 7-15.

While there may have been the possibility of Fundy one day being an 18-hole course, the original concept was for nine, and that is the reason the layout flows so well, never giving the feeling of a patchwork routing.

This was no half-hearted effort on Thompson's part. He created a stellar work, bringing into play two branches of the same stream on six of the holes. The holes work with the natural topography, and players must adjust for elevation changes and slopes throughout the round.

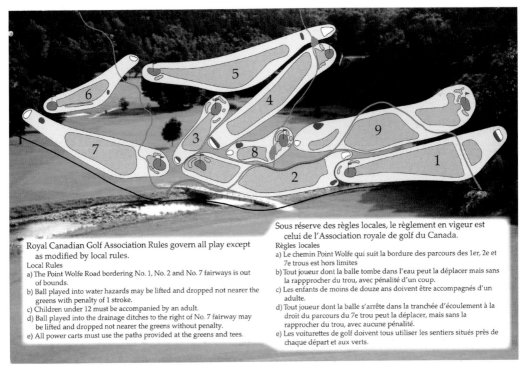

Royal Canadian Golf Association Rules govern all play except
as modified by local rules.
Local Rules
a) The Point Wolfe Road bordering No. 1, No. 2 and No. 7 fairways is out
of bounds.
b) Ball played into water hazards may be lifted and dropped not nearer the
greens with penalty of 1 stroke.
c) Children under 12 must be accompanied by an adult.
d) Ball played into the drainage ditches to the right of No. 7 fairway may
be lifted and dropped not nearer the greens without penalty.
e) All power carts must use the paths provided at the greens and tees.

Sous réserve des règles locales, le règlement en vigeur est
celui de l'Association royale de golf du Canada.
Règles locales
a) Le chemin Point Wolfe qui suit la bordure des parcours des 1er, 2e et
7e trous est hors limites
b) Tout joueur dont la balle tombe dans l'eau peut la déplacer mais sans
la rappprocher du trou, avec pénalité d'un coup.
c) Les enfants de moins de douze ans doivent être accompagnés d'un
adulte.
d) Tout joueur dont la balle s'arrête dans la tranchée d'écoulement à la
droit du parcours du 7e trou peut la déplacer, mais sans la
rapprocher du trou, avec aucune pénalité.
e) Les voiturettes de golf doivent tous utiliser les sentiers situés près de
chaque départ et aux verts.

(Fundy National Park Golf Course)

Garry McBrine is a plumber at the park and an unabashed fan of the golf course, where
he has been a member for 34 years. He and his family live about 60 miles from Fundy,
but during the park season he rents a small place by himself in the nearby village of Alma.

"That's how I get to play golf every day," he said proudly.

McBrine offers some general advice for anyone playing Fundy for the first time:
"The rough here will chew up really quickly," and "the wind blows all the time." Also,
"if the wind is at your back on the first tee you'll get wet before you go."

From the back, the Thompson design is a par-35 of 3,069 yards.

The first hole is a par-4 of 394 yards with a tee that has to be 50 feet above the fairway, giving players a spectacular view of not only the hole, but also the vast surrounding
wilderness.

The fairway is spacious off the tee, nearly 60 yards wide and 250 yards out, but can feel narrower with Point Wolfe Road and a smattering of trees down the left and a dense row of trees on the right that separates the first hole from the ninth.

McBrine said a new course superintendent cut the lower limbs off of existing trees, making recovery shots much easier, a move for which he bestowed heavy compliments.

"Here you about have to have God status to cut a tree," he said.

At the green, Thompson lets it be known that severe penalties will be meted out for those who miss the putting surfaces.

The large green has mounds three quarters of the way around it. Approximately 30 yards to the right of the first green, a long narrow bunker (the style that is found throughout Fundy) sits well above the green, benched into the slope. Behind the green, and beyond a massive hillock, sits a second bunker. Find your golf ball in either of those hazards, and, McBrine said, "just add another stroke to the scorecard."

The putting surface is one of the most level on the course.

Fundy's second hole is a par-4 of 399 yards. Point Wolfe Road continues down the left side with the stream winding its way along the right then crossing the fairway a hundred yards from the center of the green. A lone bunker can be found to the right as well as a pair behind guarding the putting surface that—like the first—has mounds on three sides. This green, though, slants severely from back to front.

"It's greasy coming down," McBrine warned.

The first one-shotter of the day is the uphill 173-yard third hole that has what McBrine calls "heaves" in the green. As with all Fundy's par-3s, bunkers have a significant impact. Here, four of the hazards nearly encircle the putting surface that is the largest on the course.

Given the fact that the sand and the mounds can cause all sorts of problems, par is an acceptable number here.

For the first time in the round, golfers will find themselves on a severely sloped fairway when they get to the fourth hole, which is 383 yards but plays much longer, as it is uphill the entire way. The fairway leans from left to right so much that drives that land right of center will not stop moving until they reach the rough.

Because of the severe hanging lie on the right of the hole, golfers on the approach shot will need two more clubs to reach the elevated green than if they were playing in from the left at the exact same yardage.

The approach shot must carry a stream 45 yards short of the putting surface. The green is also guarded short right by a large bunker and left by an oak tree. Thompson did offer a bit of a reprieve from the taxing shots required, as a gentle slope rises behind the green for a Punchbowl feature that holds in aggressive plays.

There is a bit of Fundy golf history attached to the fourth.

John D. Smith of the Stanley Thompson Society interviewed Sterling Hughes, who was part of the crew that built the Fundy layout.

According to Smith, "[Hughes] was operating a two-and-a-half-ton army truck towing around three different harrows—a disc, spring tooth, and a spike tooth—preparing the ground for top soil that was hauled in by truck. [Stanley Thompson] climbed up onto the truck and sat down (there was no top or anything on it) and started to talk to me. He had a habit of digging his elbow into your ribs to get your attention, at least with me anyway. He asked me about the course and I said I knew nothing about golf courses. He said, 'It's going to be a good one.'"

Thompson was correct.

For the fifth hole, golfers head in the opposite direction they just played, and the fairway on this hole cants from right to left.

At 481 yards and with a par of five, a birdie is a legitimate possibility, but par is always an acceptable number on this somewhat troublesome hole.

Cutting the inside corner on the tee shot, according to McBrine, shortens the hole immensely, but a miscue can mean a ball lost in the thick woods. If, though, the drive negotiates the corner, McBrine said the key to the approach shot is to play it well out to the right of the green so the firm slope can redirect the shot to the target.

Playing the fifth hole as a three-shotter is no easy task, with the fairway leaning so severely to the left.

Short, left, and well below the putting surface is the hole's only bunker. While making up-and-down from there is difficult, it does in fact prevent a worse fate. According to McBrine, missing the green long, left, and beyond the sand "is death."

Fundy's sixth hole has to stand as one of the most demanding and memorable in all of Canada. It is a jaw-dropping par-3 of 240 yards. It does, however, play downhill, the ground is firm and the green open in front to allow the run-up shot. The hole is a monster not only in length, but also because of difficulties on both sides of the broad fairway.

The hole is lined right by a forest and out-of-bounds on the right. The fairway tilts hard right to left. There is nothing good on the lower side. The best that can be hoped for is that an errant shot heading in that direction comes to rest in a 75-yard-long bunker, which sees plenty of play.

Beyond the sand there is a dense stand of trees.

"If it wasn't for that bunker there wouldn't be enough golf balls in Canada to keep people playing," McBrine opined.

Bold players will take their drives down the right side in an effort to get a favorable kick to the green. McBrine said he knows of two aces on the sixth as well as two players accomplishing a three from the tee. First they knocked their drives out-of-bounds, then reteed and holed out for par.

Most times McBrine prefers to lay up and try to make his par with a pitch and a putt; if his strategy results in bogey, that is fine with him.

"We always say if you make a four here pick up your ball and run."

A breather can come in the form of the seventh hole, a par-4 of 377 yards with a flat fairway.

The tee is well above the landing area, so the hole plays shorter than the yardage, which is an important bit of information, since a brook weaves its way through the fairway starting at 290 yards out.

Two large maples come into play on the left side, so the natural tendency is to take the right-hand option, but guarding that side, once again, is Point Wolf Road. A bombed tee shot down the right means approaching the putting surface over a massive maple, on the other side of which is a bunker at the right front corner of the green. Here, Thompson chose to build a massive mound between sand and the green, one so high that the putting surface is not visible while in the hazard.

To the left of the green, a slim bunker is placed well back. The carpet is relatively free of pitch or humps.

Eight is the final par-3 of the round and is another memorable one-shotter, playing 150 yards on the card, but the rise in the land makes it longer.

Five bunkers, all in play, wait for the mistakes. One each on the front corners are of the same style as on the seventh hole—a large knob between the sand and the green obscures the putting surface.

The three hazards behind the putting surface sit above it and require a deft touch for a successful extrication. McBrine said some bold regulars are known to putt out of them.

This is the first green on the layout that is wider than it is deep. It moves from back left to front right.

Fundy concludes with another reachable par-5, this one at 470 yards. It also is a hole that has two living remnants of the land's prior tenants, farmers.

Approximately 250 yards off the tee in the right center of the 80-yard wide fairway stands a lone maple tree. It replaced an apple tree that once occupied the exact location but died. According to McBrine, the apple had been part of the farm, and Thompson had let it remain. McBrine remembers the days when hitting the tree with a tee shot gave a player the right to hold the title of "long."

The modern "long" golfers hit well past the maple and have no trepidation about going for the ninth in two, but for those who will be playing from farther back, especially those who have hit a poor tee shot, they must reckon with the brook cutting through the fairway 140 yards from the green.

According to McBrine, laying up just over the stream is an intelligent play, as the putting surface sits well above the approach at the top of a steep rise.

"It's like walking up the wall at the Daytona 500," McBrine said of the slope.

According to McBrine, it is common for lackluster approach shots that land short of the target to race back down the hill and end up farther away than from where they were just struck.

Two slender bunkers set back from the putting surface guard the right and left front corners. On the right a huge mound between the sand and short grass blocks out the target.

Next to the bunker on the left is an apple tree, this one precariously close to the green. It is of the yellow transparent variety and annually produces edible fruit. It stands not far from where a farmhouse was once located. McBrine said a small orchard can be found amidst the thick wood line to the left of the ninth green.

Like the previous putting surface, the one at the ninth is far wider than it is deep, and Thompson closed out the round with a bit of flair. A ridge perpendicular to the line of play runs across the front third of the green, producing all sorts of treacherous putts.

Beyond the Green

You're in a National Park! That means lots of hiking trails with waterfalls. Fundy Bay has the greatest tides in the world with a mean range of about 45 feet, so you can walk on the sea floor at low tide. Pack your mask and snorkel and "swim with salmon for science" in one of the freshwater streams. The park is a designated Dark Sky Preserve, so the artificial light is kept low and the stargazing is fantastic. Be sure to bring the telescope!

CHAPTER 6

Quogue Field Club, Quogue, N. Y.

In the world of golf course architecture, it is said that the toughest piece of property on which to work is one that is dead flat.

If that axiom is true, then Thomas Bendelow had moments of genius when he designed Quogue Field Club.

Opened in 1901, the layout has less than three feet of elevation change. Stand on the first tee of this southeastern Long Island golf course, and you see nearly every hole, thanks in part to a concerted effort in recent years by the club to remove ill-situated trees that obscured views and eradicated the open feel.

If not for modern homes constructed along a distant beach, the sightline would extend infinitely south to the Atlantic Ocean and beyond.

Using teams of horses with drag plates, along with men and their picks, shovels, and rakes, Bendelow and his crew created a layout that remains challenging to this day, even in benign conditions. When the wind, though, comes off the sea, usually from the south-southwest in the summer months, Quogue (pronounced kwôg, rhymes with flog) becomes the sternest of challenges. The turf, however, is kept firm, so playing the ball below the breeze and along the ground is an option and an advisable way to confront Bendelow's design.

The features fit the land and, yet, are at the same time bold and subtle. For instance, bunkers barely visible from the fairway with just small knobs or ridges poking above the turf as hint of their existence are surprisingly deep and large on closer inspection. Greens that appear placid from a distance abound in movement.

Nearly 70 bunkers dot the layout; only the fourth is without sand pits. Except for the second and third, greens are wide open in front, their squared-off entrances at grade and welcoming to the run-up shot.

Of the 25 finest nine-hole courses in North America, Quogue's history is unique. The current layout began as nine holes, expanding to 18, then returning to the original nine.

The club was first located a mile from the present location and had nine holes of golf. When the area became too busy, Quogue relocated to the present site in 1900, and the course opened the next year. Except for the fourth and fifth holes, which were altered as the result of a religious feud, the current layout appears to have changed little in the last 100 years. There was, though, the short-lived second nine.

When golf became so popular that play overwhelmed the nine-hole layout, the club leased adjacent property and doubled the size of its course. There is no record of who designed it, but existing photos show a course chock-full of well-bunkered interesting holes. The 18-hole routing opened in 1920, and a clubhouse was built in a new location to accommodate the configuration. The original nine played as the front, with the current fourth as the first hole and the current third the ninth. Golfers then crossed Ocean Avenue to access the back nine.

After the Hurricane of 1938 decimated the new holes, the club, located on leased land, did not rebuild. The clubhouse was abandoned and the layout reverted to its original nine holes and the original routing as well, which is what exists today.

That fact that Quogue is almost completely unknown outside its immediate area is not a surprise. Residing in an upscale neighborhood, the club is located within about 15 miles to the east of four other courses—Shinnecock Hills Golf Club, the National Golf Links of America, Southampton Golf Club, and Sebonack Golf Club. Travel about four miles in the other direction, and there is Westhampton Country Club.

When Quogue opened, the layout was well regarded but was not quite at the elite level, even by the club's own admission.

". . .the new golf course with its many raised bunkers set at graceful angles, its raised tees and well turfed and shapely made greens surrounded with sand pits, was

The first green, like so many others at Quogue Field Club, rises gently from the fairway, yet within its boundaries are subtle swells and falls that will at once delight and madden. (*Anthony Pioppi*)

considered the last word in moderate priced courses, not comparable with the then existing elaborate Shinnecock Hills course, but much above average," reads the *50th Anniversary Record of the Quogue Field Club, 1887-1937.*

In October of 1901, *Brooklyn Life* magazine had this to say: "a fine golf course laid out by Bendelow—starting from the front and winding in the direction of the ocean and then to the shores of Shinnecock Bay and back to the club with bunkers and water hazards second to none anywhere on that part of the island."

Ian Andrews, the Canadian architect who is overseeing restoration work at Quogue, gives a modern interpretation of the layout:

"The moment you step on the first tee you're transported back in time to the very origins of American Golf.

"The first tee begins where the main porch ends with a long view to the ocean in the distance. The architectural features are simple, understated but cleverly arranged. There are very few experiences that can quite touch this one," he said.

The first tee is probably one of a kind among all those in golf, as a hedge borders it on three sides, close enough to give almost a cramped feeling that is in stark contrast to the wide expanse that lays before the golfer.

Hole no. 1 is a par-5 of 528 yards and brilliant in its architecture as it gently snakes its way from start to finish. Out-of-bounds is to the right, with the parallel ninth fairway available as bailout area. Immediately, Bendelow shows his skill in design. Bunkers that guard the left and right of the second landing area also play the role of making a second shot from the adjacent ninth fairway a difficult one. From that angle, the hazards take on the role as crossbunkers and through bunkers. With that touch of brilliance, Bendelow rewards only drives down the first fairway.

The green has sand left and right, while off the back is an acceptable place to have the golf ball stop.

The second is a visual stunner and a blast to play: a par-3 of 148 yards, its perfectly round slight Punchbowl green is an emerald island all but surrounded by two wide swaths of golden sand. Only a pair of narrow turf paths, there for golfers to enter and exit the putting surface, interrupt the hazard.

From the tee, finding the putting surface is difficult in the prevailing summer wind that often comes stiff from the left.

Once on the green, first-time players at Quogue can be caught off guard by how subtly the back portion rises up to a deceiving height. Downhill putts run away much more than anticipated.

The third hole maintains the high level of enjoyment. This is the first of the two short par-4s that Quogue offers, and it is a doozy at just 270 yards.

The par-3 second hole at Quogue is a step back in time. The shallow Punchbowl design that is nearly surrounded by sand harks back to the early 1900s, when it was built. (*Anthony Pioppi*)

Most likely a drive-and-pitch hole when the course opened in 1900, with a bit of luck the green can be driven by today's longer hitters. There is, however, a plethora of misfortune from start to finish, as 10 bunkers protect par, including a massive non-original sand hazard area added in the last 15 years.

Bendelow's design called for players to have the option to play down the far left side, avoiding multiple bunkers on the right including one that stretches 80 yards from the back corner of the green down the fairway rough line.

Now, though, on the left is a 50-yard-long sand hazard with six thin grass islands, sort of like Oakmont Golf Club church pews, which eliminates that play. There are multiple greenside bunkers on that side, as well. A narrow opening at the middle of the putting surface allows for the most fortunate of tee balls to make its way on. Over the back is serious trouble in the way of a salt marsh.

The putting surface is one of the more interesting. It generally moves from back to front, but there is plenty else going on. The sides are higher than the middle, and small knobs, almost indiscernible, make for some tricky reads.

The second and final par-3 of the day is not original. The bold green complex stands out in evident contrast to the other eight. The putting surface is angled from right to left and appears to be a combination of Biarritz and Redan styles, with a high bank on the right and a shallow swale running through the green perpendicular to the line of play.

The hole often plays shorter than its 191 yards, since the prevailing summer wind is at the golfers' backs. A pond on the left penalizes egregious errors. A shot that lands right of the putting surface is dead, as the approach must come over the steep-banked side.

The next two holes are part of Quogue's oddest piece of history. When the club moved to its present site, the land it chose to occupy was leased; in fact, Quogue did not buy the property the golf course is on until the 1980s.

When it opened and for more than a decade after, the club experienced no significant problems with regard to the layout. Then in September of 1913 after "a long and heated discussion," the Quogue allowed golf and tennis to be played on Sundays after 2 p.m. "but with the provision that no employees would be on duty and no caddies could be used."

Immediately, the owners of the land on which the fifth and sixth holes were located cancelled the lease. Their contract with the club contained a provision that such an action was allowable if golf was ever played on the Lord's Day.

The Sunday following the closing of the holes, golfers were met by a sign forbidding them to set foot on the grounds. A few headstrong members ripped the notice down, disposed of it, and played the holes. Later, they were called before the Board of Trustees and severely reprimanded but not punished further. For a short time thereafter, the course was played as a seven-hole layout. The 50th anniversary book recounts how Quogue rectified the problem.

"The club however did not suffer very long by the loss of the two holes, as Mr. Abram S. Post at once filled in a large section of his meadows located south of the then fourth hole and authorized the club to layout new 5th and 6th holes over such filled in area."

Quogue's current golf course superintendent, John Bradley, said the subsoil of those holes, and as a result the growing conditions, are vastly different from the rest of the layout. Apparently the fill was not of highest quality.

Along with the construction of the two holes, all the bunkers were redone. There is no record of who led the work, but the new five and six meld seamlessly into the original layout.

The fifth hole, along with the ninth, has two distinct sets of tees. It can play at 412 yards with a par of 4 or 470 yards with a par of 5. It is a heck of a hole from either location.

The defining feature is a shallow pond that runs down the left side for approximately 150 yards. The prevailing summer breeze is from the players' right, shoving tee balls and second shots toward the water. The play is out to the right in an effort to let the shot ride the wind, but two fairway bunkers and scrubby waste area on that side do not make it an inviting option.

Even with a successful tee ball, the second hole is just as trying. Bunkers pinch the landing area 80 yards short of the middle of the green, which is open in front but has sand hazards on the other three sides. As a par-4, this is the no.1 handicap hole, and for good reason.

On the scorecard, the sixth may appear to be a breather, but it is not, whether playing at 245 yards or 281 yards. The pond that was on the left of the fifth takes the same position here. The wind crosses from the pond side, pushing golf balls right toward grass hollows, or worse, out-of-bounds.

That's not all. The fairway is crowned, and even on a calm day, getting a tee shot to stay on the short grass is quite the task. When the wind is blowing? Holding the fairway is a near impossible task. Except for the front, the long narrow green has trouble all around.

Every day of the week, four is a welcome score here.

A view across the fifth green of Quogue Field Club. The home in the distance sits on the approximate site of the former clubhouse when Quogue was briefly an 18-hole layout. (*EJ Altobello*)

The same can be said of the seventh, a par-4 of 434 yards that can be a brute. Winds again are from the left, pushing tee shots to the right, where the backyards of adjacent homes are out-of-bounds. A triad of fairway bunkers also guards that side, slightly pinching the fairway, and is in play for golfers of average length.

As with eight other holes, the green is heavily defended by sand; five pits do the trick here, guarding every side but the front.

The eighth is a throwback hole to the early days of sound, thrilling, captivating golf architecture. It first played about 325 yards and was of the drive-and-pitch variety.

Now the tee has been extended back to 379 yards, a distance that gives players using modern golf equipment an accurate idea of how Bendelow's design was played when hickory-shafted clubs and gutta-percha golf balls were in use.

For the only time in this design, Bendelow placed bunkers in the middle of a fairway, doing so with a dash of stylishness as he created a "v" formation that points toward the tee. He used three sand pits to achieve the look. Bendelow mounded earth about 60 yards short of the middle of the green, then carved the hazards out of the dirt. The result is that from the tee the green, which sits slightly below the fairway, is not visible, obscured by the bunkers. From the landing area only the invariably flapping flag can be seen.

Even though the prevailing summer wind is from the right and not helping, playing well back from the bunkers off the tee just might be the smartest of choices, but there are still problems that must be faced. Bendelow, not surprisingly, has hazards on both sides of what is the logical yardage to which to lay up.

For those who can accurately bomb the tee ball, there can be a sensational reward. The firm fairway and approach of the eighth hole means that a shot that barely clears the "v" has a reasonable chance of making the green.

Overzealous efforts find a long, thin bunker that wraps the back portion of the putting surface that has sand nearly all around three sides.

Quogue concludes with a hole that can either be played as a 408-yard par-4 or a 534-yard par-5. Bendelow designed it as a par-5, so a well-played drive from the par-4 tees gets players past the bunkers he intended to watch over the original landing area.

As a five, sand guards the drive zone, while the second is hazard-free. At the final hole, though, the approach shot is where mistakes are severely penalized. Five bunkers, some of the deepest greenside variety on the course, wait to thrash any errors.

The green stands alone in relation to the other eight. For the only time in the round, two distinct tiers are found on the putting surface, with the back portion higher than the front.

The green is snuggled nearly up against the front of the golf shop and within easy viewing distance of the inviting clubhouse porch—a splendid place to relax, sip a drink, and recount the round.

BEYOND THE GREEN

You're in the Hamptons, so there is plenty to occupy your time away from golf. Chief among them is beaching, shopping, and people watching. Most beaches in the area require a permit to use, but close by to Quogue is Cupsogue Beach County Park. Along with swimming and sunbathing, the 296-acre park offers fantastic saltwater bass fishing. To satisfy your seafood craving, head to Buoy One restaurant in Westhampton, a short drive from Quogue, and let Chef Dave Girard know you are a fan of nine-hole golf courses.

CHAPTER 7

Hooper Golf Course, Walpole, N.H.

The Hooper Golf Course came very close to not making the list of North America's best nine-hole golf courses. It wasn't that the Wayne Stiles-John Van Kleek design didn't deserve the honor; it's that the facility itself was almost shut down, the result of a dizzying series of events. The course was saved, though, when in 2016 the Monadnock Conservancy purchased a conservation easement from the George. L. Hooper Trust with money raised by Walpole residents. The Conservancy embraces the golf course as open space and understands that such work as tree removal to protect the turf is vital to Hooper's success.

Meeting House West, LLC, took over running the facility in 2017. Meeting House is owned by Joe Goodhue, who lives off the seventh green and is an ardent fan of the layout. The golf course is for sale, but even if sold the conservancy will continue to oversee the property.

Like many older layouts where money was scarce for so long but respect for the course design abundant, hardly any alterations have been done to Hooper since it opened in 1928. Only a few bunkers have been added and some others reshaped in that time, but it appears the nine green sites are original and the intended strategy of the holes remains intact.

The bucolic New Hampshire town of Walpole, just off of U.S. 91, 80 miles north of Springfield, Massachusetts, borders the Connecticut River and on the far shore are the towns of Westminster and Bellows Falls, Vermont.

Stiles and Van Kleek are perhaps best known for the Taconic Golf Club in Williamstown, Massachusetts, part of Williams College. But Hooper's value remains clear.

In their book *The Life and Work of Wayne Stiles,* Bob Labbance and Kevin Mendik called Hooper "one of the finest layouts from Stiles and Van Kleek."

The charming par-3 fourth at Hooper Golf Course. When the course opened in 1928 one scribe wrote of the hole, "There is so much natural beauty that it is difficult to keep one's eye on the ball." (*Anthony Pioppi*)

There is an array of challenging holes that along the way test all facets of the golfer's game. Part of the strategic design is the rolling fairways that feature heaves and depressions and force golfers to play off uneven lies. While the routing flows with the land, the features appear to be done by the hand of man—Stiles and Van Kleek moving earth to create the best possible holes.

The June 1928 issue of *Golf Illustrated* featured a comprehensive article on Hooper's opening:

"Walpole is not a 'summer course.' The originators of the project were not content with the idea and started with the purpose of having a course that would provide a test of golf for the better players, as well as to give pleasure to the average golfer."

The purpose was met, and to this day Hooper presents a challenge to the highly skilled while remaining eminently enjoyable for the less adept.

Only one hole on the course, the first, changes dramatically depending on which tee markers are played. It plays as a par-5 of 456 yards or a par-4 of 435. Hooper, therefore, has a par of 35 or 36, and from the longer tees the distance is 3,033 yards.

The backdrop to the par-5 tee is the marvelous Watkins Tavern, a colonial mansion from 1795 that is not in use at this time but in lovely condition, its porches with views of nearly the entire course just begging to be occupied.

For the golfer, the initial hole is a harbinger of what is in store. In total, the hole falls substantially from tee to green, but along the way the fairway rise and falls in dramatic fashion. The golf ball can disappear from view on the first and second shots, sometimes to reappear again, sometimes to remain hidden until the golfer is all but on top of it. A dirt path lined on either side by stone walls, Hooper Road comes into play on the first four holes and the last two of the round. On or over the road is played as out-of-bounds.

There is a severe edge to the left side of the first fairway, and shots that miss on that side bounce a good distance away into the rough or perhaps into the dense woods.

Three large bunkers guard the green, which tilts hard from back to right, two short left and one right greenside.

Another downhill hole is the second, a par-4 of 427 yards and the most difficult at Walpole.

Again the road guards the right, along with a few large trees that stand ominously on that side. The fairway expands to the left, which is the better angle into the hole, but like the first, the fairway has a hard lip and mishits can suffer dearly.

The fairway melds into the green that is guarded left by the lone bunker on the hole, the direction in which the putting surface leans. A "4" on the scorecard here is always an accomplishment.

Golfers now step between the stonewalls and across the road for the uphill third that heads in the exact opposite direction of the first two holes, meaning the 285-yarder is extremely uphill, playing quite a bit longer than the yardage.

The green of the par-3 sixth might be the most deceiving at Hooper Golf Course. The almost imperceptible cant from the left has fooled many a player and will continue to do so. (*Joe Goodhue*)

The trouble is at the green, which is guarded in front by two bunkers, one well below the putting surface. The third bunker nestles into the mounding beyond the green.

The putting surface is markedly different from the eight others in that it is the only one on which the approach cannot be run and that is wider than it is deep. The surface tilts from back left to front right.

The club's original vice-president, Dwight Harris, may have had the hazards on the third in mind when he wrote about the construction of Hooper in a 1927 letter cited by Labbance and Mendik:

"The traps are 'whales' to fill and I am afraid will be the cause of more or less profanity from our club members and guests who get caught in them."

A par-3 of 155 yards is next. It is an uphill hole, but the severe cant of the green makes it appear less so and can fool the first-time golfer into thinking it plays to the yardage. Guarded by two bunkers on the left and one on the right, the green sits comfortably on the land in an amphitheater of tall pines.

Golf Illustrated had this to say about the hole in 1928, and it still holds true:

"The chief difficulty is correctly gauging the distance, for there is so much natural beauty that it is difficult to keep one's eye on the ball."

After a 75-yard walk through the pine stand, the player finds himself on the tee of the fifth, the second and last par-5 of the day, measuring 474 yards but with substantial decision making needed to achieve par or better.

The tee shot is uphill, and a long ball can disappear from sight over a ridge. A bunker in the right rough protects the tee for the seventh hole.

Once the hill is crested, a view of the green and the deep valley before is revealed. There are four bunkers that must be dealt with, especially for those attempting the bold play of reaching the putting surface on the next shot. Two, one on each side of the approach between 15 and 20 yards from the front of the putting surface, are formidable hazards. Once inside them, only the flagstick can be seen. The other two bunkers flank the left and right front of the carpet, which leans from back to front.

With the green perhaps 20 feet above the valley floor, those playing a short approach from there will only see a portion of the flagstick. Navigating the fifth as a three-shot hole and laying back before the valley allows more of the putting surface to be seen but leaves the player with a downhill shot to an uphill target.

The trickiest green at Hooper is found on the par-3 sixth, a hole of 194 yards that plays across the same valley that runs through the fifth.

A chain of four bunkers lurks before and along the right side of the green, while there is one on the left, the favored side from which to come in if landing the tee shot short and letting it bound on.

Here's the rub—the green cants markedly from back to front, and that is easy to discern. What goes unnoticed due to some odd optical illusion is how severely the green also banks from left to right. What look to be flat putts are in reality uphill. Whether this was an intentional design of Stiles and Van Kleek will probably never be known, but it surely adds to the fun and challenge of the sixth.

A delightful hole is the 311-yard seventh, which features two original fairway bunkers that sit just inside the right and left rough approximately 80 yards from the green and are very much in play. It is the only time during the round that the architects squeezed a landing area.

Five bunkers guard the putting surface, more than on any other green at Walpole. There are two on the right and one short left of the putting surface. In a quirky twist, two sand pits are carved into a plateau left of the green and sit all of five feet above the carpet, which is set into the land in sort of a Punchbowl style.

Finding the elevated sand hazards is easily done, but hitting a successful downhill recovery shot from there is not.

In order to get to the eighth tee, golfers must take a 135-yard stroll on a path along Watkins Road. They eventually arrive at the tee of the eighth hole, a downhiller of 381 yards. It presents few problems on the right but is guarded the entire way on the left as Hooper Road returns to play a role in the design. The defense of the eighth is at the green, the left edge of which sits a mere eight yards from the stonewall over which is the road.

Sometime in the 1990s, two bunkers were added, one between the green and the wall, probably to reduce disasters on the approach shot, as well as one on the right of the putting surface.

Hooper concludes with a testing par-4. Approach the green from the right, and two bunkers dominate the eye and affect decision making. (*Anthony Pioppi*)

Golfers cross Hooper Road for the last time to face the finishing hole, a tester even at 350 yards.

From tee to green there is a decided ascension of the land. Hooper Road stands watch on the left side with plenty of room to bail to the right, so naturally the best play into the green is from the side fraught with trouble.

To the right, a ridge frames the fairway. In the mid-1990s, two bunkers were added in the rough but are ill-suited to the design.

At the left front of the green is one bunker, and on the right two intimidating sand hazards wait. Those golfers who play in from the right and want to go directly at the green must carry both bunkers, which can also shield the putting surface from view.

Those who avoid the bunkers and play to the right of the green will find themselves with a testing chip or putt to a putting surface that runs away from them. Coming in from the left, the green is welcoming.

After playing Hooper, it is easy to come away with the feeling that the course has hardly been modified in its nearly ninety years of existence. The reason for that is the amazing foresight of the founders. Written into the original bylaws is a rule that states the board of governors has to approve "substantial changes" to the course.

Harris may have been the impetus behind that idea. In the same letter from 1927, he wrote, "I am sure we will eventually have a most beautiful course not only from the scenic side, but from the playing side. And we must see to it that we not only make it a good course, but keep it so."

When Hooper first greeted players, it reached back to the earliest days of organized American golf, as recounted by *Golf Illustrated:*

"The opening ceremonies had a touch of the historical when Frank H. Allen, of New York, a summer resident of Walpole and one of the country's oldest golfers, was the first to drive from the tee. He is the only surviving charter member of the St. Andrews Club of Yonkers, N.Y., reputed to be the oldest in the country."

BEYOND THE GREEN

Walpole Academy is on the National Register of Historic Places. The former school is now a historical society museum.

There is also the Walpole Mountain View Winery as well as the Distant Hill Gardens, an environmental learning center that boasts 58-acre gardens.

L.A. Burdick Chocolate, with locations in New York City as well as Cambridge and Boston, Massachusetts, has its home store in Walpole.

Walpole Village Tavern is the place for a sandwich and a local craft beer.

Of course, there are several farm stands and organic farms in the area.

CHAPTER 8

Cohasse Country Club, Southbridge, Mass.

Think of a Donald Ross-designed nine-hole layout in Central Massachusetts, and the name Whitinsville Golf Club should immediately come to mind. It is, after all, the finest nine in North America.

From now on you should also think of Cohasse Country Club, which is also among the best nines on the continent.

Located approximately 20 miles west of Whitinsville in Southbridge, Massachusetts, Cohasse has remarkable similarities to WGC. In fact, Cohasse may have served as the inspiration for Whitinsville.

Cohasse is a private Donald Ross layout that was commissioned by the town's wealthiest family, industrialists who formed the private—but not elite—club for those who made a living in and around their factories. The same is true of WGC.

In Southbridge, that family was the Wells brothers—Albert, Cheney, and Channing, owners of the American Optical Corporation, the largest manufacturer of ophthalmic products in the world at the time. In Whitinsville (pronounced *White-ins-ville*), a section of Northbridge, Massachusetts, it was the Whitin family (pronounced *whit-in*), founders and owners of Whitin Machine Works, at one time the largest maker of specialty textile machinery in the world.

Both companies long ago shuttered their doors to the buildings that once housed thundering machines and thousands of workers. These buildings are now home to small businesses, storage units, and in one case a hotel, but the most prevalent tenants are the ghosts of better days.

Like Whitinsville GC, Cohasse is one of the last remnants of a thriving New England mill town, a surviving testimonial to the wealth and generosity of those who conceived and built the golf courses.

The official founding date of the club is July 13, 1918, when six holes were playable. For the event, the Wells brothers invited 200 guests and essentially turned over the

Find your golf ball one hundred yards from the center of the first green at Cohasse Country Club, and you have three routes to get the ball home, two via the ground game and one through the air. (*John Mallon*)

facility to members of a country club that was yet to form but would be made up by the invited guests. The first members were doctors, lawyers, and accountants, but also AO managers and mill workers, who not only golfed at the club, but also swam in the pond and played tennis on the new courts.

It was a fine layout to begin with, but upgrades occurred in 1927 and 1930, perhaps in reaction to Whitinsville's superiority. Walter Hatch, a construction engineer for Ross, was brought in to improve the course through the addition of bunkers and the conversion of a par-3 to a par-4.

The membership also hired the finest landscape architecture firm in the country, the Olmstead Brothers, to improve the beauty of the entranceway as well as the area around the clubhouse and locker rooms, although their plans might not have been implemented.

The Cohasse course of today is extremely similar to how it looked when Hatch put on his finishing touches in 1930. It is an exacting layout that in no way feels outdated and that can be enjoyed across almost all skill levels. The routing includes one of the only times Ross incorporated back-to-back par-3s.

Cohasse plays 3,051 yards from the blue tee markers. The men's par is 35, while the women's is 37.

Yet even with this relatively short layout, Ross displayed his acumen. None of the holes can be considered a pushover, and many of them have the ability to convert one bad swing into a double bogey or more.

Cohasse opens with a wonderfully intricate hole of 427 yards that gives golfers three routes to reach the green, each calling for precise shot making.

The most obvious is for the long hitter to play from the elevated tee down the left side of the fairway so that the green is open for a second shot directly to the putting surface.

The second method involves the slightly shorter hitter again taking the tee shot down the left side, but laying up on the second, since any shot that runs through the green either climbs a steep bank and nestles into the rough, leaving a dicey chip, or falls off the back, again into rough, where a deft pitch is the only form of recovery.

The third option, and the most intriguing, is also for the player who lacks length. After a drive to the center or right side of the fairway from where the green is hidden, the approach is played over a fairway bunker to the top of a knob. With the correct kick, a golf ball can bounce and roll a good 40 yards down the slope and find the smallish putting surface that tilts from right to left.

Hatch added the lone bunker that guards the green in 1927.

Where the first hole rewards the longest player, the second hole negates their strength, demanding an accurate approach and exacting a stiff penalty for failed efforts.

The 342-yard hole begins with a downhill tee shot, but a brook about 245 yards out that runs across the fairway removes the advantage of length, since gnarly rough lies beyond. The second shot is uphill some 20 feet to a volcano green, the putting surface perched atop a hill where shots long, left, and right will be sent caroming or bounding away, leaving a virtually impossible up-and-down to a green that cants severely back to front.

Ross designed a narrow approach to the green, but tree encroachment on the left side of the fairway has negated that option.

The third hole is a daunting par-3 that can play as long as 202 yards. Four bunkers—three that are greenside—flank the target, which tilts from back left to front right. There is another element to the third hole that oftentimes makes playing the hole much more of a challenge: a gallery.

To the left of the putting surface is the pro shop, outside of which members often congregate. Above and to the left of the putting surface is the practice green. Off to the right is the first tee. Then there are the assorted folk that wander down from the nearby restaurant to watch a little golf. Not a good hole for golfers averse to crowds.

Turns out the third hole was just a warm-up for playing in front of judging eyes.

The second consecutive three-par is the 132-yard fourth hole that is also a Volcano Hole. But unlike the second, the shot to the green is downhill.

Bunkers that guard the left and front were added by someone other than Ross or Hatch. Come up short of the front sand pit, and the ball will run 30 feet back down the steep slope until it finds the small pond, which explains why early members nicknamed the hole "Kerplunk."

The tiny two-tiered green of the Cohasse's fourth hole is difficult enough to hit on its own. The fact that diners in the nearby restaurant are peering over your shoulder makes the task even more demanding. (*John Mallon*)

The small green is two-tiered, with the back about a foot higher than the front and the shelves slightly angled to the line of play.

Oh, and the wind nearly always swirls around the green and tee, making it impossible to ever be confident of the club selection.

If all that is not enough to put a golfer on edge, then one merely needs to look behind oneself before playing the hole to realize he or she is the live entertainment for patrons in the restaurant's main dining room who were lucky enough to get a window seat.

Go ahead—glance, smile, and nod to the appreciative gallery before turning back toward a green that now appears minuscule.

Make a three or better here, though, and you have achieved an accomplishment that will have earned the respect of the fans and the golf gods.

A walk across Eastford Road takes you to the weakest hole at Cohasse, the uphill, 90-degree dogleg left fifth of 327 yards that presents one prudent play off the tee, a shot of 180 to 200 yards that will come to rest on the severe upslope of the fairway. From there it is a short iron to a treacherous green.

When the course opened, and for many years afterwards, the tee was on a higher location back and to the right of where it is now, and the conifers on the left of the fairway were much shorter, creating the option to carry them. Now that play is impossible except for the longest and highest of hitters.

Most of the green cants hard back to front, with the rear third more level. Bunkers flank the left and right corners.

Being above the hole almost guarantees a three-putt, or worse, a putt-chip-putt scenario.

The only par-5 on the course is the sixth hole, and two bunkers on the 544-yarder were added by Hatch.

Off the tee the play is to the right of the tilted fairway, so shots roll left, down to the level portion. Get caught in the right rough, and a severe hanging lie results.

From here Ross and Hatch turned up the strategy.

A fairway bunker just left of the centerline dominates the eye and is very much in play, especially for shorter hitters and those who found the rough left.

For those golfers who do not possess exceptional length, the layup shot takes thought and precision. Fifty yards short of the center of the green is a brook. About 45 yards short of the brook, a downward slope starts. The fairway from the ridge top down to the brook is canted severely right to left. The object, then, is to land the second shot on the slope so that it bounces and rolls to a safe location away from water and rough.

In a genius bit of strategic planning by Ross, laying up well back from the brook means hitting an approach shot from a stance with the ball above or below your feet.

Even off a flat lie the play to the green is not a simple task.

The two-tiered putting surface, with the back portion higher, sits some 15 feet above the fairway. A bunker is located to the left and a severe slope guards the front. Any shot short of the green will run 30 or more yards back down the fairway, possibly into the stream.

Birdies can be had, but sevens and eights are also common.

From there, Cohasse ends with an entertaining trio of par-4s.

The seventh hole was originally a 217-yard par-3 that Hatch extended to a par-4, with the green being doubled in size. The hole now plays 325 yards.

In the 1930s, when Cohasse built the new back tees, the club was unable to determine after a thorough search who owned the needed land. The club, though, still went ahead and extended the hole, hoping the rightful owners when found would be willing to sell the small parcel, which apparently they did.

Eastford Road, which runs the entire length of the seventh on the right, is out-of-bounds. Two fairway bunkers to the left capture the tee shots that were played too far away from the trouble. There is also a sand hazard short right of the green.

The bunker positioned at the front left of the putting surface obscures a view of the green from the left, but in a splendid touch of strategy the golfer who flirted with the dangerous right side is provided with a clear look at the carpet.

The green, one of the largest at Cohasse, has the least tilt of any on the course.

The 250-yard shaded walk from the seventh to the eighth hole is a delightful one that takes golfers back across Eastford Road and along the edge of Cohasse Pond. A building where the pump house is now located served as a swimmer's changing area when the club first opened.

At 388 yards, number eight is a hole that gives the golfer two lines of play. One is to hug the left side and carry the hill for a level lie on the approach. Take that route, though, and the landing area is blind from the tee. The alternative is playing out to the right for a longer second. The problem with taking this option is that while the fairway

In September of 1925, Charlie Fitts took a break from mowing the sixth fairway to be photographed. (*Cohasse Country Club*)

is visible, it tilts hard to the right and sends shots away from the line of play, many of which find the rough.

Two cross bunkers left and short of the hole as well as two right green-side bunkers loom large on the uphill approach that plays at least one club longer than the actual distance. A stone wall and an out-of-bounds area are devilishly close to the back of the putting surface that inclines from back left to front right. It is advisable to keep all shots below the flagstick.

Cohasse ends with a downright cool, quirky par-4 of 374 yards that with the right skill level, the correct course conditions, and a little luck can be driven. The nine, though, is also capable of inflicting a double bogey or beyond with the mere crack of a tee shot.

The hole plays markedly downhill for 180 yards or so and then rises up to a ridge about 240 yards from the tee, the same ridge that affects the tee shot on the eighth.

A tee ball carried far enough has a chance to run down the acute slope to the green that is the most severely tilted on the layout, running back to front.

Bashing driver rather than laying up, though, presents a bevy of problems. A triad of bunkers resides in the right rough, and beyond them is worse trouble, a parking lot. (Important note: if you ever play Cohasse, park as far away from the ninth fairway as possible.)

Players can also bail left into the eighth fairway, but a perfectly positioned bunker off the left corner of the green must be negotiated on the approach.

For the shorter hitters or those who lay up, the approach shot is dicey. First of all, the green is blind. The ideal target line is often a chimney on the roof of the clubhouse that is just off the back edge of the green.

The second problem is deciding whether to use the slope and run the shot onto the green or to fly it there.

Almost any shot that stops past the hole is a guaranteed three-putt. An unusual little v-shaped mound that Ross built is positioned to the right of the green, a cool feature with which Ross concluded the round.

Beyond the Green

Notre Dame Church on Main Street is worth a stop for fans of building design. It is the work of prominent Canadian architect Joseph Venne.

There is also the Optical Heritage Museum that meticulously traces the interesting history of American Optical from a one-man operation to the world's largest manufacturer of optics, including the AO's role in the development of fiber optics, originally a secret CIA project aimed at coding messages.

That same building houses The Cannery Music Hall, which attracts regional and national acts.

If seafood is your desire and the restaurant at Cohasse cannot satiate your want, then search out Fins and Tales.

CHAPTER 9

Aetna Springs Golf Course, Pope Valley, Cal.

It was late in 1882 that an ill, prominent San Francisco lawyer, Len D. Owens, was restored to health by the magic waters at Aetna Springs, 85 miles north of the city.

So enamored was he with curative powers and the lovely surroundings of Pope Valley that he bought the property, constructed a hotel, and created the Aetna Springs Resort.

The area had once been the center for the mining of cinnabar, from which mercury is extracted, and then used in gold production. In its heyday, there were 3,000 working mines in the region, but when Owens first visited the boom was over.

Owens's idea was a success, and for more than fifty years, until the family sold the property in the 1940s, the elite and common man of San Francisco journeyed there. Owens's endeavor was described by the *San Francisco Chronicle* in the July 30, 1894 issue:

"These are delightful midsummer days and nights at this nearby summer resting-place, where the time is pleasantly parsed in sweet idleness or in walking, driving, dancing, swimming or hunting, as the varying of the fancies of the guest dictate. There is a soothing sense of security in this elevated resort, hemmed in by the mountains clothed in perpetual green."

The people came for the restorative qualities of the water that they bathed in and drank. Owens, ever the marketer, even had the water bottled and shipped to the city.

In the early 1900s, jumping on a fad, Owens's guests could also partake in the "grape cure" that was sweeping Europe and the US. It involved eating the grape, seeds, leaves, stems, and stalks as a means to end all sorts of ailments.

In an amazing bit of luck for Owens, his daughter from his first marriage, Frances Marion, became one of the highest paid screenwriters in Hollywood, winning two Academy Awards along the way. She often visited her father's resort and brought with her the likes of well-known actors such as Mary Pickford and Lionel Barrymore, which served to increase its visibility and reputation.

The names of the non-Hollywood famous who journeyed to Aetna were noted in the weekly newspaper gossip columns under headlines such as "Society Folk at the Resorts" and "Society Goes to Country Places by Automobile."

Somewhere along the way, perhaps as early as the 1890s, Owens put in four tiny golf holes. Owens later claimed that they were the first in California. They were not.

The real golf course, a nine-hole affair, opened in 1921, and Owens announced the addition in a *Chronicle* advertisement that was honest about conditions:

"Nine-hole golf course now finished. This being first season, fairways are not very smooth, but this is a very sporty course, all natural hazards. Putting green on one of our lawns, also nine hole clock golf on one of the big lawns."

Even though the 1926 and 1927 editions of *The American Annual Golf Guide* listed Aetna as a 5,000-yard 18-hole layout, it remained a nine with some modifications along the way as holes were added and abandoned. For most of its existence, the greens were oiled sand.

Eventually, the resort fell on hard times and was all but abandoned. Then in the mid-2000s a developer arrived with an audacious plan—upgrade the existing layout and revive the resort. On a huge nearby parcel of land, 18 more holes and other resort amenities would be built. That dream, though, came to a sudden and definitive halt when the county would not grant the needed permits for the new course.

Work stopped immediately, creating a surreal scene. Resort buildings dating to the 1890s that were undergoing improvements are still partially sheathed in white plastic that ripples in the wind; some that had been lifted off their foundations might remain so for years.

Before the county's decision was handed down, though, the architecture team of Tom Doak and Jim Urbina created an entirely new Aetna Springs. It was Urbina who was on site and oversaw the construction.

The resort is 16 miles from the nearest real municipality, Middletown. Pope Valley is little more than a general store and auto repair shop. Hills, cattle, fields, and grape vineyards surround the layout and the new, comfortable clubhouse. The spring that brought folks looking for a cure no longer produces the mystical water.

The course is at once fun and formidable, without being brutish. For fans of the work created by Doak and Urbina, the greens have less movement than most of their other designs. Still, all classes of golfers will enjoy the strategy the pair created.

Aetna plays to a par of 35 and is 3,057 yards from the back tees.

The first hole is one of the most—if not the most—strategic on the golf course, with a length of 369 yards and a par of 4.

One must cross a small stream in order to get to the green. The more dangerous of the options allows for the longer hitter to carry water on the tee shot and on the approach. The prudent play, especially when it is the first hole of the day, is to lay up off the tee and to fly the hazards on a longer approach.

The green is two-tiered with undulations that will test putting skills. There is ample room to miss left and past the putting surface.

The second is a long, level par-3 hole of 228 yards. The same watercourse that had to be dealt with on the first hole again must be carried here. The putting surface tilts back to front, with ridges dividing it into three distinct sections. A lone bunker guards the right front, but players can play short or left of the green with little or no problems.

History is a significant part of the par-4, 372-yard third hole. A stream brook runs down the first half of the fairway on the left side. Deep and heavy rough awaits the golfer, and a left fairway bunker is also well placed. The bailout is to the right, but two bunkers make the play a bit tricky.

Because of a natural rise in the land, from the left side of the fairway the green is not visible, but the flagstick can be viewed. From the safe angle on the right neither can be seen.

Like all the holes at Aetna Springs, the third sits comfortably on the land. To the left of the fairway remains the shell of a building where the curative water was bottled. (*Anthony Pioppi*)

A springhouse dating to the earliest days of the resort also sits to the left. Stop to look, and water is still visible. The story goes that it was here that the Owens's famous elixir was bottled for customers that longed for better health.

The green rises from the front leading to a pronounced back shelf.

When Urbina and Doak were looking to place their holes, a notch where the fourth now sits appeared to be a natural location. From tee to green, the 134-yarder

The short fourth hole. During construction a sand and oil green was discovered in almost the exact location where the existing putting surface is located. (*Anthony Pioppi*)

sits in between a ridge dropping sharply from the right and another from the left; a wash runs along the right side of the hole. There is a bunker short right of the green and another carved deep into the left slope above the putting surface. Set off by itself, a good distance from the third and fifth holes, the fourth has a cozy, serene feel to it with the sun playing through the trees and grass-covered hills visible in the distance.

They were not the only ones who found this spot ideal for a par-3. According to Urbina, during construction a perfectly round sand-and-oil green was unearthed in the exact spot where the existing putting surface sits. It was not part of the existing course when Urbina arrived on site, and it was never determined when the historic green was in play.

The entire fifth hole, all 338 yards of it, is visible from the tee that sits high above the fairway. This includes the stream that is almost exactly 100 yards short of the green, the landing area it divides, and the sharp incline that leads to the putting surface, which is guarded on the right by a protected species of native oak.

The decision then is whether or not to lay up short of the water. An approach shot will play a club to a club and a half more, just due to elevation.

The play into the green should be a shortish shot with accuracy required, since anything that does not make the plateau can come back down the hill a good 50 yards. A shallow falloff behind the green will send golf balls that skip off the back into the dense rough.

The green offers no trickery, so birdie putts are to be had if the approach was on point.

Six is a hole that can play much shorter than its yardage of 395 yards because 60 yards short of the middle of the green the fairway falls sharply toward the putting surface.

More protected oaks can give a slight cramped feeling off the tee, but the fairway is generous in its width, over 65 yards in some spots.

From the falloff in the fairway to the green, the hole corridor opens up, but two oaks on the right cause plenty of problems for those looking to run the ball in from that side.

The green has two small knobs and leans away from the line of play, encouraging the run-up approach as a result.

The green site is perhaps the most tranquil spot at Aetna, with grasslands and hills just beyond. A nearby wooden rail fence just about begs to be leaned on.

Between the sixth and seventh holes, Urbina and his crew uncovered a second oiled sand green. Unlike the one on the fourth, it had sat uncovered for decades under the blazing California summer sun, turning to the consistency and color of pavement.

More charming views await from the tee of the seventh hole, including the valley floor and surrounding hills. At 425 yards, seven is rated the most difficult hole on the course.

It bends to the right against a hill that falls to the left. The play is to take the tee ball around the corner in order to play the approach into the open side of the green, but oaks guard the favored route.

A vineyard runs along the left side of the seventh hole on the tee shot, but the fairway opens up, leaving a massive bailout area on that side.

While an approach shot can be run in from the right side, from the left side, getting to the green requires carrying two bunkers carved out of the base of the fill pad. Another bunker sits beyond the putting surface.

Hole eight is the only par-5 at Aetna, and it is one that calls for thought and shot making from beginning to end.

The hole is divided into three sections by a pair of streams that forces the longest of hitters to make choices on the tee shot. First is whether or not to lay up. If the answer is to go with the driver, the second decision is where to hit it.

The left side of the hole is guarded the entire way by out-of-bounds, with a road and fence serving as reminders, but it is from that angle that the green is most accessible.

If the play is away from the trouble, the tee shot to the right and onto the second section of the hole must carry one of the streams. Going too far right, however, will result in trees blocking the route to the green.

For those who kept the driver in the bag as well as shorter hitters, the second shot also has its quandaries. The fairway narrows, guarded on the left by oaks and on the right by more oaks and a pair of bunkers, approximately 75 yards from the putting surface.

Eight concludes with a largely flat green, although there is a subtle mound in the middle right portion. The surroundings are bunker-free.

At 293 yards, the finishing hole is the shortest par-4 at Aetna. Because of a pair of bunkers placed on the line to the green, only the longest of hitters will be able to go for it from the tee, since a shot of 270 yards is required to carry the sand. It also must be a precise drive, since oaks left and right pinch the fairway. For good measure, out-of-bounds is also on the left side.

If the goal is to end the day with a good score, then forgoing the driver and opting to play the hole as a two-shotter will more often than not lead to par or better.

BEYOND THE GREEN

In Calistoga, if barbecue is your thing, then Buster's Southern Barbeque is a must. One bit of advice—the warning about the hot sauce is not to be disregarded. If gambling is a favored activity, then Twin Pine Casino & Hotel is the spot. It often hosts live entertainment, as well. Twin Pine is about a 30-minute drive from Aetna Springs.

CHAPTER 10

Fisher Island Club, Fisher Island, Fla.

Fisher Island is all of 216 acres located no more than 350 yards south of Miami Beach, and maybe 240 yards south of Dodge Island, home to the Port of Miami. Yet it is one of the most exclusive locales in the United States. The 2010 U.S. Census listed it as having the highest per capita income of any place in the country. The population is about 300, and the private island is only accessible by boat or a small private ferry.

As for the club itself, it has roughly 650 members that call nearly fifty countries home. NHL players, oil barons, movie moguls, and captains of industry spend time here in the winter, and those who golf do so on the P.B. Dye layout that opened in 1989 and that Dye updated in 2007.

The two-parcel layout sits on 42 acres. Holes 1-5, 8-9, the driving range, and practice greens comprise one piece, with holes 6-7 located a four-minute golf cart ride away. The layout, which rarely feels constrained, plays to a par of 35 tipping out at 3,069 yards.

A barrier island, Fisher was formed in 1905 as part of a dredging project by the US government that created the Government Cut shipping channel. The tip of the Miami Beach peninsula was lopped off in the process and became what is now Fisher Island.

In 1925 Carl G. Fisher, for whom the island is named, traded Fisher to William Kissam Vanderbilt for his yacht, *Alva Base*.

It wasn't until ten years later that Vanderbilt initiated moving to the island when architect Maurice Fatio drew plans for the mansion that Vanderbilt named after the boat. The home, described as a "getaway bungalow," and two nearby cottages, all of which have Mediterranean Revival exteriors, did not open until 1940. Vanderbilt died in 1944 and shortly after his wife sold the property.

Over the ensuing decades ownership of the island, which maintained much of its native vegetation, exchanged hands a number of times. It was not until the early 1980s that development of Fisher began.

Now there are condominiums, which sell for an average of $6.5 million, a fifteen-room hotel, six villas, four historic cottages, and a guesthouse with five suites. Rooms start at about $1,100 a night. The mansion is home to two restaurants, conference rooms, a saltwater pool, and a billiard parlor.

There are seven restaurants on the island, eighteen tennis courts, a health club, an upscale market, a spa, and a beach club for which white sand from the Bahamas was imported. There is also a fire department, grammar school, and bank. There is a place to park the yachts and another place to anchor the *big* yachts.

It might be difficult to believe that Dye was able to find a way to lay out a nine-hole course that exceeds 3,000 yards, never mind one that never has the players feeling cramped or has holes playing too close to each other.

Although there is only one hole directly on the water, nearly all of them afford views of the ocean, the routing heads to the four major points on the compass in the first five holes; all of those holes also have out-of-bounds down the right side.

The first, at 330 yards, calls for a right-to-left shot off the tee and the opposite on the approach, nothing too difficult.

Five bunkers guard the green, three to the left, but there is plenty of room to miss short and right and a wide avenue to run the ball onto the putting surface.

"I'm just trying to get them out on the course" is how Dye described his thoughts regarding no. 1.

At 435 yards with out-of-bounds down the entire right side, the second is a test. Dye designed a rolling fairway, and it adds to the drama of the hole. The green is a reverse of the first. A cluster of bunkers sits to the right of the putting surface, but the left side is open and accessible via the ground game. Two more sand hazards guard shots that go long.

The pitch of one of the larger putting surfaces on the course runs from back right to front left.

Barely visible, but just to the right of the hole, is the Fisher Island tennis complex, notable due to the fact that all four surfaces of the Grand Slam venues—the U.S. Open, French Open, Wimbledon, and Australian Open, can be played there, including the red surface of Roland Garros.

The third hole is all of 130 yards, but it is best described as a knee-knocker. The tee shot is entirely over water to a green whose width is greater than its depth. A knob in the back middle makes putting there interesting.

There is one bunker long left. Palm trees and megaexpensive high-rise condos loom over the hole. Just a touch of moving air will make club and target selection even more difficult.

Hole number four heads directly north toward South Beach. The 450-yard par-4 that plays directly into the prevailing winter wind has out-of-bounds down the right side, but the fairway opens up to the opposite side and that is the ideal angle from which to approach the green that is perched above the fairway and has severe fall-offs on three sides. The only bunker that would affect an approach shot is approximately 45 yards short of the middle of the putting surface.

Golfers standing on the tees on the fifth hole will see before them one of the more unusual views in all of golf. It is here that the course first runs parallel to Government Cut and across the water is the Port of Miami. On a quiet day, the massive cranes used to lift cargo stand erect and silent. On busy days, however, hulking faded red freighters as well as gleaming white ocean liners inch their way toward their destinations or sit rolling dockside as their cargo is loaded or unloaded.

Once concentration returns to the fun at hand, one discovers that Dye produced an unexpected wrinkle. The 375-yard hole actually plays downhill, a neat trick on an island that has no discernable elevation change. The digging of two irrigation ponds produced the soil to create the fall. Dye also incorporated humps and bumps into the fairway so that even well-placed tee shots can end on an uneven lie.

The green of the short third hole at Fisher Island Club. Palm trees and multimillion-dollar condominiums stand watch. (*Anthony Pioppi*)

A massive bunker fronts the putting surface that is wider than it is deep. There is a small bunker to the left and a good-sized one at the back.

One must use a golf cart has to get to the next two holes, six and seven.

The original routing of the two was changed when a dock for a small cargo ferry was built. The auto traffic to and from the dock made the original routing a bit too dangerous for golf carts.

The current sixth is a pleasing hole to the eye and has a par of three. From the back markers the tee shot on the 173-yard hole is over an irrigation pond. To the left is the seventh hole, Government Cut, and the Port of Miami. The green sits beyond a wooden bulkhead. A narrow strip bunker between the bulkhead and the green starts in front of the putting surface and wraps all the way left around the peninsula on which it sits; palm trees add to the hazard on the left.

The green is large, but tame.

Risk and reward is what the seventh is all about. Wrapping left around the pond, it plays 382 yards on the card. Interestingly, if one believes Google Earth, the closest part of the Port of Miami on the right is only 273 yards away. Docked cruise ships will be much closer! A row of palms, though, prevents testing Google Earth's accuracy by firing a tee ball or two at the behemoths.

The conservative player who hits a straightaway tee shot of 225 yards will be in business. What players must account for in picking a target is the prevailing wind out of the right pushing shots toward the pond and a bunker that separates it from the fairway.

The bolder player who wants to bite off a portion of the water must fly a drive no less than 240 yards. A well-played shot, especially one that turns right to left, can catch a zephyr and bound its way toward the green, leaving a flip wedge as the golfer's last play. At the same time, the tee ball that flies too far will find a bunker, if lucky, and if unlucky, will fall out-of-bounds.

An approach, especially downwind, is not a simple assignment. The green is slightly elevated above the surrounds with a quick steep rise from the fairway to the putting surface. The pond and bunker sneak in on the left. The right side is open, but a bunker not visible from the fairway sits hidden beyond.

From there, golfers return via the golf cart to the main portion of the course and the final two holes.

Before getting to the eighth tee, it is possible to take a detour to the island's aviary, which houses over a dozen species of exotic birds, including a flock of flamingos.

Dye describes the eighth hole as "a short four that is blind," but the hole is so much more than that, a sought-after mix of quirky, fun, and challenging.

One of Fisher Island's year-round residents on the seventh tee with the sixth green in the background. (*Anthony Pioppi*)

From the back tees the hole is 271 yards, and what causes the green to be out of view is a Bermudagrass volcano-like structure that rises out of the fairway to a height of about 15 feet. The massive, dominating feature is reminiscent of the unusual seventh hole at Ocean Links, the long-gone Seth Raynor-Charles Blair Macdonald nine-holer that bordered Newport (R.I.) Country Club for a short time beginning in 1919. That hole was 272 yards and played over a man-made mountain with an odd-looking aiming slot in the top.

Fisher Island's eighth has no such feature, but carved out of the apex of the mound is a bunker adding just a tad more risk for the golfer attempting to reach the green in one shot. A second shot from the elevated sand is a downright weird experience.

In an effort to avoid the hill, laying up down the right side is an extremely risky play because of a pond and a strip bunker.

Going to the far left is only slightly better. Three small, round bunkers guard that side.

For good measure, Dye added one bunker in the downslope of the mound and two, one on each side, guarding the most undulating putting surface at Fisher Island.

The sum of all the parts is a hole that can be easily birdied, parred, or bogeyed—and a blast to play.

Nine is the only par-5 on the golf course. At 523 yards, it is a reachable affair.

The entire right side of the hole is lined with white out-of-bounds stakes. The generous fairway bows sharply to the right approximately 220 yards out. On the right side is the aviary as well as a corner-guarding bunker.

Those choosing to lay up on their second shot will find an open and receptive portion of fairway. However, players electing to go at the green in two will have a pair of bunkers with which to contend.

Forty yards short of the putting surface, smack-dab in the middle of the fairway, is a deep, round sand hazard looking to inflict a severe price for not carrying it.

To the left of it, the side from which to best approach the green, is a larger bunker positioned in the rough. The green has one bunker on the left and right.

The centerline bunker can distract from the task at hand for the golfers firing at the carpet on their third shot. For those golfers who can maintain their focus, the green is welcoming.

Once the sun sets, golfers might find themselves returning to a particular location next to the ninth hole. It is there that the Victor Arsidi Observatory is located, providing views of the heavens.

Beyond the Green

Seriously? If you are on Fisher Island, finding things to do should not be a problem. If the island itself does not provide enough entertainment, Miami and Miami Beach are a short ferry ride and then drive away.

CHAPTER 11

Norfolk Country Club, Norfolk, Conn.

In 1926, A.W. Tillinghast journeyed to the northwest corner of Connecticut to lay out a 9-hole golf course for the Norfolk Country Club, which at that time only had tennis as a formal recreational activity.

It was quite the achievement to get Tillinghast there. He was considered one of the finest, if not *the* finest, architect in the country, with designs that included the recently opened layout at Baltimore Five Farms, the two courses at Winged Foot Country Club, and Baltusrol Country Club, as well as the expansion and nearly complete overhaul of Newport (R.I.) Country Club.

In 1924, he had designed his only course in Massachusetts—Berkshire Hills Country Club, located approximately 40 miles directly north of Norfolk in the then-thriving mill town of Pittsfield.

At Norfolk, which formed in 1912, Tillinghast was up against the competition, literally. NCC bordered the nine-hole Norfolk Downs Golf Club—one of the first public golf courses in the country—that was owned by the extremely wealthy Bella Eldridge. For years, Norfolk Country Club members played at the Downs but then tired of Eldrige's steadfast rule of no golf on Sundays and wanted a layout of their own.

The Downs was short, even for that era, listed in a 1905 *Hartford Courant* article as just over 2,000 yards, with an abundance of movement thanks to the natural topography. There were seven par-4s and two par-3s. Though the design was highly touted in a *Courant* article (as seemingly every course was by publications of that era), the Downs went fallow in the early 1940s after the inheritors of the facility decided not to continue operations.

At Norfolk CC, Tillinghast left behind a solid, fun layout that would have exceeded the quality of its elder neighbor, and the course of today appears to be very close to the one that opened in 1927.

Only two significant alterations seem to have occurred. In the mid-1930s, the first green was moved back about 100 yards to its current location, and as a result, the third hole was changed from a dogleg left to a straightaway hole.

The opening tee shot of Norfolk Country Club, an A.W. Tillinghast design. All the trouble is left, but bailing to the right makes the hole significantly longer. (*Christopher Little*)

On two other holes, a pond and a bunker were added over the years but did not substantially alter the strategy.

Norfolk opens with stern challenges on the first two holes. Number 1 is probably the most demanding hole on the course, a 490-yard dogleg left that drops severely from the tee to the first landing area, then rises abruptly from there to the second landing area, where a level lie is rare.

Here, the golfer faces the first significant decision of the day: go for the green or lay up. There is no easy answer, since white out-of-bounds stakes line the entire left side of the first hole, as they do on four other holes, and much of the first part of the fairway leans toward those imposing little posts. The reward for choosing the long club is the chance to chip and putt for birdie on the opening hole, a grand way to start the day. The penalty is at least a double bogey.

The green sits between two large mounds and, like seven of its siblings at Norfolk, is cantered back to front. Like the eight other kin, there are subtle knobs and hollows throughout the putting surface.

The second is a difficult uphill 170-yarder that plays 10 to 15 yards longer because of the rise from tee to green. Bunkers are placed left and right of the putting surface. Out-of-bounds is left. The "miss" is in front, and it is always better to be below the flag than above it because of the severity of the pitch of the putting surface.

Factor in a bit of swirling wind, and par is acceptable each and every time one plays the hole.

The third hole provides golfers with what could be considered the first (much-needed) breather, although trouble is close at hand.

The 255-yard, straightaway four par originally played into the green from the right, but the angle was altered to accommodate the lengthening of the first hole. Now, players going directly for the putting surface with driver face trouble left in the way of out-of-bounds, while trees create issues on the right. Even though the hole is short, laying up is a pragmatic option.

A sizable bunker, large enough to grab a player's attention, wraps around the right and back of the green and, with a touch of flair from Tillinghast, serves as a hazard for the adjacent fifth green, as well.

The fourth hole is a 350-yarder with a severe drop from the tee almost to the green, which is nestled with the axis pointing left, indicating the best side from which to play the approach into the hole. A shot that winds up long and off the back can fall some 10 feet below the putting surface, making for a testing recovery.

It is a fun design that tempts players to swing from their heels to get every last yard out of the drive and significantly shorten the hole in an attempt to make birdie, well aware of what comes next. Not the most prudent strategies, but understandable.

After that, golfers turn 180 degrees and play up the same slope they just came down. The fifth is a par-4 of 425 yards, but thanks to the hill it plays well over that, closer to 460, making it essentially a par 4 ½.

The fairway is generous in width, but no matter, because even after a crack tee shot, the second is fraught with trouble.

The bunker, shared with the third hole, guards the left of the fifth green. The good news is that OB is long. Because of the severe pitch in the putting surface, any ball that comes to rest past the hole leaves the golfer with a problematic putt, or two.

For fans of golf course history and/or golf architecture, at this point in the round, it is advised to walk off Norfolk CC, over the wall, and onto the remnants of Norfolk Downs.

Immediately behind the Country Club's sixth tee is the former fourth green of the Downs. The fill pad and bunker shells are easily identifiable; the greensite sits no more than 15 yards from the tee of the Country Club's sixth hole.

When both courses were active, that area served up quite a view. NCC players could look down at much of their course, while the Downs golfers looked up from the 216-yard hole called "Edgewood."

According to the July 26, 1905, *Hartford Courant,* the hole had "practically the only level fair green (fairway) on the course, having only one small hollow into which the ball may accidentally fall. At this point on the Downs, the course turns and winds its way back nearly parallel with the ground already covered only a short distance between, making it possible for the anxious onlookers of the game to watch a number of the players driving from the tees on hills and putting on the different greens during the tournament."

How old is this sign? At one point, two golf courses were located on Mountain Road. One, Norfolk Downs, has not existed since the early 1940s. (*Anthony Pioppi*)

Once the historic walk is over and players are back on NCC, they are faced with the intriguing downhill par-4 sixth hole. The length is only 360 yards, but this is no pushover.

Again, out-of-bounds is down the left, while a large natural ridge running a good portion of the fairway on the right divides this hole from the previous one.

Tillinghast appears to have given the shorter or more conservative players a break, hollowing out a section of a landing area to create a forgiving Punchbowl. Off the tee golfers who bail to the right away from the out-of-bounds stakes are likely to get a favorable bound that will direct their tee ball to the middle of the hollow. Some 20 yards beyond that area, though, is a portion of fairway that appears to have been flattened—reward for the longer hitter who chose the bold move of hitting driver and/ or staying away from the right.

Tillinghast skillfully infused the approach to the green with a heavy bit of strategy. The putting surface is angled from the back right to the front left. The fairway on the left is angled toward the green, and a smartly played approach that lands in the correct area just short of the green will carom onto the welcoming putting surface. To pull that off, a golfer must direct the shot toward out-of-bounds in order to get the favorable kick. Those shying away from the challenge might see their approaches bound hard and away to the right. Those who are too bold will end up in a narrow back bunker that guards almost the entire back of the putting surface, an addition that came well after the course opened. The original Tillinghast design had no such barrier and was much more severe. Golf balls over the green would have found dense woods and then most likely been lost.

At the seventh hole, a par-4 of 350 yards, the golfer for the first time in the round sees a dead flat hole stretched out in front of his or her unbelieving eyes.

There are two ponds down the left side. The one closest to the tee, which was added well after Tillinghast designed the course, is in play only for a duffed shot. The second pond is an integral part of the simple strategy—the closer one's tee ball is played near the water, the better the angle into the green.

There is trouble down the entire left side, and long as well, where a ball off the back of the green could easily find swamp.

As would be expected, Tillinghast creates a more difficult approach for the player who avoided the water.

The par-3 eighth hole at 140 yards is the least interesting hole on the course, and a bit baffling in its design.

The green sits slightly higher up than the tee, making the hole play longer than the scorecard indicates. The putting surface is so severely banked back to front that any shot that comes to rest in line with or beyond the cup is almost a guaranteed three-putt, even with NCC's fair green speeds.

Tillinghast could have nestled the green complex against a hillock to the rear, creating a natural Punchbowl, but ignored the option.

Norfolk concludes with a delightful and quirky hole with an unusual hazard in play.

The minuscule ninth green, surrounded by trouble, sits just below the Norfolk Clubhouse. (*Christopher Little*)

The ninth is but 250 yards and ends at a minuscule green that is perhaps no more than 1,400 square feet, and that is nearly ringed with bunkers.

Those going for it in one have problems to the right and left. To the right is a steep falloff that sends golf balls bounding away until they end up somewhere on the first hole. A recovery shot from there is blind.

The miss left, though, is much worse. Four tennis courts, which are reachable even though fencing and shrubbery are in place to protect them, are adjacent to the green. A shot that is well left of the fairway but short of the tennis courts is no bargain. It results in a blind approach that must be played over the courts, no easy task to begin with but made even more difficult when matches are underway.

Norfolk's golf professional, Ron Pfaefflin, says the best way to approach the hole, and one that he preaches to the two high school golf teams he coaches (Northwest Regional 7 and Gilbert in Winsted), is to read the yardage out loud before teeing off, "two hundred AND fifty yards . . . two hundred AND fifty yards."

In other words, hit it two hundred yards off the tee, leave yourself 50 yards for your second, and a four can be carded, or maybe even a birdie three. Take the aggressive alternative, and a five, six, or worse is easily made.

The fact that Tillinghast laid out Norfolk was completely forgotten for decades until club member Michael Kelly was researching the book he authored, *The Country Club Norfolk Connecticut, 1912-2012*.

First he came across letters from Arthur Knox, who led the club's efforts to build a course and was one of ten members who donated a combined $25,000 to accomplish that goal.

Knox wrote how he traveled to New York to meet "the best golf course designer in the entire world" and returned with him to Norfolk.

According to the information that Kelly uncovered, Knox related how the allegedly Scottish designer "never drew a sober breath" in all their time together.

While combing through board minutes, Kelly discovered the mysterious "Scot" was none other than Tillinghast, an American and a well-known drinker.

According to Rick Wolffe of the Tillinghast Association, Norfolk comfortably fits into Tillinghast's other work of that period.

"In the mid-1920s, he was working with what nature gave him," Wolffe said. "There wasn't a lot of earth moving. He just followed the natural terrain."

Kelly also found that in 1935 Tillinghast returned to Norfolk during his nation-wide tour on behalf of the PGA of America, during which he gave architectural and agronomic advice to clubs. Tillinghast walked Norfolk CC and the Downs and created a routing that would combine the two into an 18-hole layout if the Country Club decided to purchase its neighbor, which was for sale. The transaction, though, never came about, and as a result the Downs reverted to forest and the Norfolk Country Club stands as the eleventh best nine-hole golf course in the US and Canada.

Beyond the Green

Northwest Connecticut has a plethora of nine-hole layouts if you want to go in that direction, including the Hotchkiss School Golf Course, ranked twenty-fifth among North America's best nines.

Literally right next door to NCC is the Norfolk Curling Club. Clinics begin in September.

Norfolk is also the home of the Yale School of Music and Norfolk Chamber Music Festival, which runs throughout the months of July and August.

CHAPTER 12

Glenboro Golf and Country Club, Glenboro, MB, Canada

There is a slice of golfing heaven just outside of Glenboro, MB, Canada, the kind of landform on which every architect dreams about laying out a course.

It is here that Glenboro Golf and Country Club is found.

This is the same type of terrain that Perry Maxwell fell in love with when he journeyed to Kansas to build his Prairie Dunes Golf Club (originally nine holes) and the design team of Bill Coore and Ben Crenshaw fawned over when they first viewed what would become Sand Hills Golf Club in Nebraska, considered by most to be the best golf course built in the Modern Era.

This dunesland, 35 miles southwest of Brandon, Manitoba, and formed eons ago, brings to mind some of the finest linksland of the British Isles with its majestic rolls, humps, dips, and swales. It is ideal land on which to hit and pursue little white spheres, as all the while the winds whip over the Canadian prairie much the way the legendary courses are buffeted across the sea.

According to club lore, Glenboro was created by a group of early members. Then, greens were comprised of sand and waste oil. They were not converted to grass until the late 1960s.

The often-repeated tale, though, might not be true. If there was someone with design knowledge who advised on or possibly even laid out the Glenboro course, the name had long been forgotten.

The second green of Glenboro Golf and Country Club sits atop the natural contours of the extraordinary dunesland on which the course was laid out. (*Troy Sigvaldason*)

There is a tantalizing bit of evidence to suggest that Glenboro's design has roots from the home of golf.

For the club's 50th anniversary in 1977, Allen Green wrote a brief history, interviewing the older members for the piece. One recounted how shortly after its election the Glenboro executive committee went to the Brandon municipal course for help in laying out the holes. The man in charge of the Brandon course, "a good Scottish fellow," volunteered his services and came to Glenboro for three days. In that time, and with local help, he laid out the nine holes. "He remarked that the course was the closest setting to a Scottish course that he had seen in Canada," recounted one member in Green's history.

Patrick Law, an assistant golf professional at Shilo Country Club (also in Manitoba), grew up playing Glenboro. He may have unmasked the mysterious Scot. In researching the founding of Glenboro, he has anecdotal evidence the man was James Pringle, a Scottish pro who had been hired away from Linlithgow Golf Club outside Edinburgh by Brandon Golf and Country Club in 1921. Two years later he moved to the Alcrest Club in Winnipeg, which is no longer in existence.

A newspaper article from 1923 details Pringle designing two nine-hole layouts in Manitoba.

"He has done a certain amount of golf course architecture being responsible for the layout of the Souris course, and last fall he laid out the course of the Beaches Golf Club at Winnipeg Beach, which will be opened for play this season," reads the piece.

The Beaches is long gone. Souris survives.

Whoever it was—Pringle or someone else—knew what he was doing. Glenboro, at just over 3,000 yards, is formidable and yet fun with its array of holes that utilize the land forms to their utmost and yet has only two bunkers. Greens are on the smallish side but present an array of styles.

"It ticks all the boxes," said Canadian architect Riley Johns, codesigner of Winter Park Golf Course, the twenty-third best nine-hole golf course in North America, and an unabashed fan of Glenboro.

The original routing at Glenboro had the current second hole as the opening hole. When the clubhouse moved, the original par-3 ninth hole became the first. The downhill hole of 176 yards has two trees right off the tee and another pair at the back corner of the green, which tilts back to front and has a steep falloff to the right. Missing the putting surface to that side virtually guarantees a bogey or worse.

It is here that the Glenboro neophytes will get their first taste of wind, which will most likely be coming hard from the right on this hole, and what dramatic effect it can have on the flight of a golf ball.

While the second hole may seem to be an easy one at 325 yards, even into the wind, making a four or better requires skill.

The longest of hitters can reach the upslope leading to the elevated green, but that can mean an awkward stance for the short shot that comes next. The putting surface, blind on virtually every approach shot no matter the distance, is of a Punchbowl style and set back in an enclave of tall pines. Once on the green, straight putts are rare.

It is on the third hole that one of the dominant themes of Glenboro displays itself. The tree-lined 405-yarder is a straightaway and straight downwind affair, but it is the undulating fairway that can determine the difficulty of the second shot, since it does not often yield flat lies and demands golfers adapt to uncomfortable stances. A quirky green adds another line of defense. The interior of the small, flat putting surface is the most benign on the course, but holding it is difficult, as all the way around the edge falls off severely.

Playing the opposite direction of the third, and back into the prevailing wind, the fourth hole is the only par-5 on the course, totaling 523 yards.

The entire left side is out-of-bounds with poplar and spruce guarding the right and making the hole feel much tighter than it is. At 250 yards out, the hole corridor is 60 yards wide.

The defining attribute of the fourth hole, though, is a large gully running through a good portion of the fairway that makes for a difficult stance on shots into the green.

"See the trend?" Law asked of the fairway contouring.

An acute back-to-front tilt of the putting surface helps to stop approach shots while at the same time making for difficult downhill or sidehill putts.

Hole five is the final one-shotter at Glenboro and a stern challenge at 211 yards. It's the first hole that plays with the wind at the player's left.

The fairway rolls and surges before melding into a relatively tame green.

Much like the second, the sixth hole is a short par-4 (337 yards) where the longer golfers have to contend with troubles reserved just for them.

Lay back with a drive of less than 220 yards, and the fairway is flat, but beyond that is a slope gradually rising to the putting surface that is filled with knobs and depressions.

The magnificent rolling fairway of Glenboro's fifth hole reminds one of the great links courses of Great Britain and Ireland and is indicative of the terrain on which the course is routed. (*Troy Sigvaldason*)

A narrow row of trees can be found down the right side of the fairway, beyond which is the seventh hole. Send a tee shot far to the left, and reaching home in two is out of the question, as a stand of poplar trees prevents a shot to the green that is one of the most interesting at Glenboro.

Law describes it as having "a large flat portion on the right, as well as a steep, well-defined ridge that guards the back and left as it winds through."

He said having to traverse the ridge adds a significant degree of difficulty to two-putting or making an up-and-down.

Seven is a straight par-4 of 379 yards, but plans are in the works to extend the hole and make it into a dogleg left par-5 with the tee shot emerging from a shoot of trees.

For now, hole seven has out-of-bounds down the left and the sixth hole on the right side. The average and shorter hitters will find a welcoming landing area, but take it too far, and large heaves and pockets are found the rest of the way in to the putting surface. The green is protected in front by a terrific centerline bunker, the first sand hazard of the day and one of only two at Glenboro. The carpet cants hard from right to left, the most severely pitched green on the layout.

Even with the wind at the golfers' backs, the 371-yard eighth is a rigorous test.

"This is a truly challenging hole that sits perfectly in the routing to either make or break a round or match," Law said.

He speaks from experience, having more than one stellar card "broken," as he calls it, by the hole with the no. 1 handicap.

It marks the only time of the day that the golfer is faced with a significantly tilted fairway, as this one leans hard to the right for a good portion. Miss right of center on the tee shot, and the golf ball will most likely find the tree line, thus eliminating any chance of going for the putting surface on the next shot.

To avoid having to produce such a precise tee ball, many Glenboro regulars will lay back to a flat area and leave themselves a much longer, uphill approach from a deep depression in the fairway.

Then there is the green. Miss left, and the golf ball runs a good distance away, resulting in a tough up-and-down.

An error to the right can catch a slope that will usher shots onto the green, but shots that go beyond the forgiving kick slope end in dense undergrowth.

The most difficult hole deserves a diabolical green, and the eighth has just that, as the putting surface tilts acutely away from front left to back right.

Nine's tee box is on the site of a slice of Glenboro history. Not long after opening, the club hired a fulltime greenkeeper, and, realizing he needed a structure out of which to work, members built the first clubhouse on the location of the ninth's back tee. A clubhouse expansion years later required a different site.

Coming at the end of the par-5 fourth hole, the back-to-front slant of the green can help those players looking to reach with a long second shot. (*Troy Sigvaldason*)

The hole is 293 yards, and the fairway contrasts with every other one at Glenboro, in that it is flat.

The hole doglegs sharply to the left at about 245 yards, and it is there that a feature not usually found on a links golf course comes into play.

A narrow stand of tall spruce trees juts into the line of play. As a result, even players who land in the left portion of the fairway find that they have no shot to the green on their next shot, as the conifers block the path. Longer hitters, however, can fly the trees off the tee and reach the putting surface.

The final target is slightly above the landing area. Golfers who on the tee shots bailed to the right must carry a bunker on their approaches.

Two tiers define the green. The smaller back portion, two feet above the front, has some of the best hole locations at Glenboro. When the flagstick is there, up-and-downs are hard to come by.

It is because of the small greens that Law and others who regularly play Glenboro have such strong short games.

"It's something we grew up dealing with, and didn't realize what a pain it was," he said.

BEYOND THE GREEN

No trip to the Glenboro area is complete without spending time with SARA the Camel. The 17-foot-high, one-ton George Berone sculpture represents Spirit Sands, more commonly known as the Manitoba Desert that is located six miles north of town in Spruce Woods Provincial Park. The park, according to the official website, "has unlikely plants like the pincushion cactus and strange creatures like the hognose snake."

CHAPTER 13

The Course at Sewanee, Sewanee, Tenn.

For more than eighty years, The University of the South was content to have as its campus golf course a quirky, short, and entertaining nine-hole layout that had small, flat greens, few bunkers, and a couple of drivable par-4s. Then in the mid-2000s, the winds of change swept over Tennessee's Cumberland Plateau and The Course at Sewanee as it existed was deemed passé. The prestigious school hired one of the hottest golf course architects in Gil Hanse, and he transformed the layout into a modern design, extending the course yardage, building new larger greens, and adding penal bunkers throughout. The only inkling of the old layout that remains is the shuttered clubhouse located on the way from the eighth green to the ninth tee.

The new holes may have names (Valley of Sin) and features (Principal's Nose Bunker, renamed Bishop's Nose) that refer back to the classic linksland courses of the British Isles, but for this project Hanse channeled his inner Robert Trent Jones. Every hole could be classified as—in the often-repeated words of Jones—a difficult par and an easy bogey.

This is by far the most demanding layout in the list of the twenty-five finest nine-hole North American courses. It is so tough, as a matter of fact, that on a few holes the gold tee markers are regularly relocated from their intended tees forward into the rough or the fairway to make those holes manageable for the golfers who play from them.

A clarion call to all golfers who play Sewanee is trumpeted at the first hole, which is rated the toughest on the layout that plays 3,068 yards with a par of 36.

The opener, called Alps, a classic links name, is a par-4 of 463 yards or par-5 of 556 yards.

Hanse by no means eases players into the round.

The landing area is minuscule, somewhere between 25 and 35 yards wide with trees left and right. On the way into the hole, the fairway drops off considerably before rising sharply to a green complex that is pure RTJ.

Approximately 150 yards from the green's center and on the right side of the fairway is a huge bunker dotted with grass islands.

The putting surface is much wider than it is deep, meaning an approach shot with a long iron, hybrid, or wood might not hold the green.

Oh, and for those looking to run the ball onto the putting surface, good luck. There is a narrow opening on the right side on which a shot could be bounced, but about 75 percent of the carpet is guarded by a bunker whose floor is six feet below the green surface.

Hanse's penalty for the shots that go long is a steep, rough-covered bank. It takes a bagful of talent or a generous portion of luck to get a shot from there to stop on the green, never mind snuggle up to the hole.

From there, players take a 180-degree turn and encounter the par-5 second hole that plays 533 yards, where the tee shot is played over wispy rough and a blow-out bunker.

On the downhill tee shot, the longest of players will be laying up, especially if the second is playing downwind, as a brook runs across the fairway at approximately 290 yards. For most golfers, the stream that sits in a low point between the first and second landing locations cannot be reached with a driver.

The second shot is vital to get correct because a tall, lone tree guards the right portion of the green, and two bunkers—one left, and another on the right—constrict the landing area about 130 yards short of the putting surface. There is also a large tree in play on the right that should have been taken down during the renovation. Golfers who find themselves in the right fairway bunker, which in a cool bit of design flair can also come into play on the fourth hole, must play over, under, or around the offensive tree.

The green of the third hole of The Course at Sewanee accurately illustrates a prevailing theme of the Gil Hanse redesign: miss the putting surface, and the price paid is steep. (*Photo courtesy of The Course at Sewanee*)

The green on the second hole is long and narrow with short being the only safe place to miss with the approach shot. On the left, a large mound runs the length of the putting surface. To the right and long, missed shots will catch the downgrade and run well away from the intended target.

The third hole is the first one-shotter of the round and is an absolute bear, playing between 140 and 188 yards. If forgiveness is, as Alexander Pope states, "divine," well, the third has not an ounce of godliness. It does, though, have one heck of a view.

From the tee, players have no depth perception, as the horizon is the Tennessee sky. The drive cannot be run onto the green; the aerial game is insisted upon, a trait right from the RTJ playbook. Tee balls coming up short find sand, as do ones that miss left and back left. Anything long right will find the nearby forest, and a shot off the right side will kick away, easily ending up 35 yards from the middle of the putting surface, which tilts back to front.

The good news is that after holing out, players are presented with a wonderful view of the Cumberland Plateau.

Respite might be found in the drivable fourth hole that plays 246 yards. To make a good score, whether going for it in one or laying up, all shots must be spot-on.

The downhill hole is well bunkered, including one in the left fairway that acts as an aiming point. Carry this one to catch a slope that just might direct a tee ball to the green. Three bunkers guard the right of the putting surface, including the one that is also in play on the second hole.

Missing short of the green or left of the green is satisfactory. Long, though, is death in the way of scrub brush and the stream that cuts through the second hole, as well.

Still, birdie is a reasonable goal here.

The fifth, much like the third, is an uphill par-3, but where the second had an infinite horizon, here a lone tree gives the golfer a bit of feel for the shot. Much like its sister hole, however, the fifth does not treat kindly the errant tee shot.

The place to leave the tee ball is short of the long, narrowish green that features a hump on the left front that can direct shots away from the planned target. Left of the putting surface is rough and then beyond that thigh-high grass. Slightly off the back is sort of OK, but well long is a tangle of grass. Then there is the right side. Miss on that side, and just walk straight to the sixth tee because that is most likely where the golf ball will stop rolling. Hey, the good news is you can leave your clubs right there as you try and make up-and-down.

The fifth hole of The Course at Sewanee leaves almost no room for error. It does, however, offer expansive and stunning views. (*Photo courtesy of Course at Sewanee*)

There is delightful viewing of the valley from this green, as well. Spend a moment taking in the sites.

The new sixth, a tough four par of 437 yards, is nothing like the short, quirky drivable four that once occupied the site.

With the Hanse configuration, all you need to do to avoid trouble is hit a great drive and not make even a slight error on the approach shot.

The fairway cants hard right to left toward Shakerag Hollow, and a ball played too far left will surely find the woods that lines that side of the hole. The right side is tree-lined, as well, and a fairway bunker on that side is in play for the golfer who hits it shorter than most.

Bending to the left as it nears the hole, the fairway has a bunker near the centerline, 45 yards short of the green's front.

The Hanse putting surface sits in a hollow and the shot into it may not be of great length, but the surface is fiercely guarded by sand.

A lone bunker guards the low (left side), while a devilish pair await on the right. The recovery from those two requires a sand shot to a green that runs away from the golfer, so the chance of holding the putting surface vacillates between slim and doubtful.

From there it's onto the par-4 seventh hole that extends to just over 400 yards but is by no means a breather.

The tee shot is fraught with danger. Like the sixth, the fairway leans to the left but not quite as severely as the previous hole. In the left rough, 190 yards into the hole, a bunker awaits. There is another 240 yards out from the tee and is located in the right rough, designed to entrap golfers looking to use the cant of the fairway to their advantage.

The shot from the sand pit to the green is made more difficult by the fact that that shot might have to be played under a tree that serves as protection from tee shots on the eighth hole.

This is no easy undertaking, especially with the land short of the green sharply angled toward thick woods short of the green. A left greenside bunker can serve to snag a shot that might otherwise be lost. Right of the green is acceptable, but long is an awful place to be.

The eighth hole plays as a short part four of 315 yards and also a medium two-shotter at 370 yards. The largest sandy waste area on Sewanee is right in front of the tees and adds aesthetics to the hole.

The Bishop's Nose feature determines the strategy, and leaving the tee ball just short of it results in a downhill approach of approximately 130 yards. Since the land banks hard to the left, staying right of that bunker complex is the favored route. Carrying the feature offers little reward, since the green cannot be driven. It is an island amid six bunkers, and so the approach shot must be of the aerial variety.

The walk to the ninth hole takes golfers past the newly upgraded hotel, the expanded tennis area, and the old clubhouse.

Like the opener, this hole can play either as a par-4 (478 yards) or a par-5 (513 yards). Called "Road," it is patterned after the famous seventeenth hole at the Old Course in St. Andrews, Scotland.

A tree to protect golfers on the first hole and a fairway bunker that would be easily flown are on the right. On the left are more trees and beyond them, Green's View Road.

Whimsical mounds in the fairway add fun to the hole. The green and bunker complex fit the Road Hole mold. Approach shots can miss left, right, and, for the only time in the round, long. Two well-played shots, and a birdie four could certainly be the final number posted on the card.

BEYOND THE GREEN

A short drive away is Sweetens Cove Golf Course, ranked as the second-best nine-hole golf course in North America. Playing Sewanee and Sweetens back-to-back is one of the best daily doubles there is.

University of the South's campus is worth taking the time to stroll through.

The Sewanee Writers' Conference is held each summer on the campus and is funded by an endowment from the estate of American playwright Tennessee Williams, who left his literary rights to the school.

Attendees of the twelve-day conference take part in workshops, readings, panel presentations, and lectures.

CHAPTER 14

Birchwood Country Club, Westport, Conn.

Birchwood Country Club has a history that might be unique not just to the best nine-hole courses in North America, but also to nine-hole layouts anywhere.

One of the first courses in the country to be conceived and constructed after the Second World War, Birchwood was built on the site of a former eighteen-hole layout, the Westport (Conn.) Country Club. Architect Orrin Smith, though, had pretty much totally disregarded the previous course, eschewing almost the entire layout except for a portion of one hole. Smith knew what he was doing. Birchwood, from commencement to conclusion, is a laudable design.

Westport opened its doors in 1912 as a nine-hole course before expanding to eighteen in the early 1920s. It ceased operation in 1943 when a bank foreclosed on it.

Sometime later, the property was purchased and the idea for Birchwood was hatched.

According to the club history, "the group attempted to establish a completely non-sectarian club and members of the entire general community were invited to join."

Later it adds, "this section of Connecticut was barren of any county club which freely admitted members without regard to their religious faith."

That concept, however, was not embraced.

As a result, Birchwood, according to the club history, became the second Jewish club in the state.

Smith, a Connecticut architect, was hired to design the layout. His work would be familiar to members, as he had designed the 18-hole Longshore Country Club in Westport, originally a private facility but now owned by the town.

Smith designed mostly in the New England-Mid Atlantic region and honed his craft as construction superintendent for two acclaimed architects, Donald Ross and Willie Park, Jr.

The Birchwood routing works down from the clubhouse and then gracefully moves along the rolling terrain until the ninth rises up for the formidable finish. At no point in the round do consecutive holes play in the same direction. The course measures 3,336 yards from the back and has a par of 36.

The first hole, a sharply downhill dogleg par-4 of 399 yards, is the only time at Birchwood that Smith somewhat followed the routing of the Westport CC layout. The corridor is much the same as a hole from the previous course, but Smith set the green site well away from the original version.

The putting surface is fabulous, sort of a modified shallow Punchbowl. The green pitches up from the fairway to a middle plateau with the left and right side tilting toward the center. The back portion, in a clever twist, runs away from the middle of the putting surface.

Smith follows the first hole with an uphill par-5 of 537 yards that plays a good 20 yards longer and calls for accuracy. The first landing area is narrow, and a miss to the right can send a shot careening down the severe slope.

From there the fairway drops slightly before rising sharply to the green. About 110 yards out from the putting surface, two bunkers are tucked into the left rough guarding the preferred angle from which to approach. One long bunker to the left and two bunkers to the right defend the putting surface.

After a downhill and uphill hole, Smith gives the golfer a nearly level one at the third hole, where almost the entire 349 yards are visible from the tee. With firm conditions and a tail wind, longer players can get close to the putting surface, but that is not always the correct choice. A large bunker guards the front while two smaller ones guard the left and right. The pushup green falls abruptly off the back.

The first green at Birchwood Country Club is probably the most interesting, with movement and intricacies not found anywhere else on the course. (*Anthony Pioppi*)

The advisable approach to the putting surface that is full of subtle rolls might be a full wedge rather than a delicate shot over sand. The rolling fairway, though, does not provide many level lies, a wonderful characteristic Smith incorporated into the third.

Number four is a par-3 of 165 yards that plays a bit shorter, as the green is below the tee.

The putting surface is set diagonally to the line of play with a large bunker that is lower than the green guarding the front portion. A narrow strip bunker guards the left. Go long, and the golf ball could end up on Riverside Avenue.

At the fifth hole, the drive is level on the 396-yarder, but the green is above grade and calls for some calculation on the approach. Here, Smith allows the ground game to be used, as the land was worked to create a kick slope that will direct the deft shot onto the green. A bunker guards the right front of the putting surface, which leans left to right.

Six is the no. 1 handicap hole on the golf course, an uphill dogleg right of 413 yards made far longer by the fact that tee shots land on the rising fairway and get little or no roll. Try to cut the corner and fail, and a lone bunker and trees await. Bail too far to the left, and there is more of the same, sand and trees.

The land falls and then rises just before the green—seemingly a simple little design feature by Smith to help the long run-up shot reach the putting surface, which is guarded on the right by a long bunker and on the left by mounding and then a bunker.

Birchwood concludes with a 3-4-5 finish starting with the seventh, a hole of 194 yards that rewards length and accuracy. The green is shaped like a guitar pick, narrower end nearest the tee, and protected short right and left by a pair of deep bunkers. The putting surface leans from back to front and is receptive to long, low shots.

Beyond the green to the left is one of the few remnants of the previous layout. The straight line of trees once lined the hole corridor of Westport CC's eighth.

The final par-4 of the round is a doozy, 383 yards that begins with a dramatically downhill tee shot followed by a dramatically uphill approach to a green that appears to be the size of a soup can lid. The fairway narrows at about the 250-yard mark with trees on the left and a triad of problems on the right—a bunker, gully, and out-of-bounds.

Getting to the green will mean using more than one extra club because of the significant upslope. The putting surface is guarded short and right by a large bunker and left by a slightly smaller one. A small rough-covered mound arcs around the back half of the green, making for some nasty lies on shots that trickle off the carpet.

Birchwood concludes with an excellent par-5 of 499 yards, short enough to beckon the longer golfers to try for the green in two while providing enough strategy to hold the attention of those electing to play the ninth as a three-shot hole.

The play off the tee is seemingly simple, straightaway and slightly uphill. On the left, though, is a line of trees and on the right out-of-bounds stakes, on the other side of which is the driving range. There are few more humiliating golf experiences than having to ask a group of fellow golfers to pause in their practice in order to retrieve a wildly wayward shot.

Architect Orrin Smith designed a superb finishing hole at Birchwood. Whether going for the par-5 green in two or three shots, the ninth provides plenty of rewards and punishments. (*Anthony Pioppi*)

In order to get to the green with a second blow, the ideal angle is in from the left. The fairway falls gradually then rises abruptly to a green of moderate dimensions. A bunker 30 yards short of the putting surface is wedged just into the left rough, and another bunker is placed a little farther up on the right. Still another sand hazard can be found left of the green. Thick rough from behind and right of the putting surface makes for a difficult recovery.

For those taking three shots to find the putting surface, the task is not a snap. The green is well above the fairway with only a portion of the flagstick visible from below. The knowledge that going past the hole will make for a tricky two-putt adds to the pressure. If the approach is from the right side, there is a large, lone tree, an outcrop of ledge, and a bunker that must be carried.

From there, the walk to the historic clubhouse is a short one. Josiah Raymond constructed the original building in 1790.

An interesting note on Birchwood's history is that one of the greatest amateur golfers to come out of Connecticut and one of the finest American amateurs ever is a former member. Dick Siderowf won his first of two British Amateurs and was a Walker Cup member while playing out of Birchwood. The victory came at Royal Porthcawl Golf Club in Wales. He would win again three years later at the Old Course in St. Andrews, Scotland. Siderowf also played on four Walker Cup teams and captained another.

Beyond the Green

Westport, one of the wealthiest towns in one of the wealthiest regions of the country with a history that dates back 7,500 years, was home to Pequot Indians. Europeans settlers arrived in 1693. Check out Compo Beach if chilling and catching some rays is what's needed after a round of golf. An abundance of restaurants and shopping is within a short drive.

If teeing it up some more is on the itinerary, check out the aforementioned Longshore Country Club.

CHAPTER 15

LivingStone Golf Course, Calgary, AB, Canada

Sometime in the mid-1990s, Ron Goodwin flew over an area west of Calgary and spied a remarkable portion of the landscape replete with ridges, valleys, streams, and ponds. It was, he correctly deduced, an ideal spot for a golf course.

Goodwin found the owner of the property and purchased the needed acreage. Then, he and two sons, Mike and Brent, set about designing and building the layout, their first such project. It opened in 2014 as LivingStone Golf Course and immediately attracted golfers from the region—and for good reason.

LivingStone plays 3,200 yards with a par of 36 from the black markers with monstrous carries on a few tee shots, far enough to challenge the longest of bashers, but the other three markers—red, white, and blue—demand no such skill. First and foremost, this is a family-friendly layout, built for the ranchers and locals looking for an entertaining diversion and some exercise.

It's for that reason, superintendent Dave Landry said, that there is not a single bunker to be found. The lack of sand is not for ease of maintenance, but for "ease of golf," according to Landry.

In the eyes of the Goodwins, the water features, the topography, and the wind appropriately add challenge and penalize miscues.

"This is not a championship course," Landry said. "That's not what they wanted."

Let's be clear, though, LivingStone is not a pushover. The design balances the qualities of testing and entertaining.

"It's just a really fun round of golf," Landry said.

According to him, the spot where LivingStone is located has an inexplicable vibe to it, which he noticed shortly after starting work there in 2016.

"You feel like something is here, the land, the ridges, I don't know what it is," Landry said.

He's not the only one. He recalled what one regular told him, "I feel rejuvenated when I play here, even if I play the worst round of my life."

Canadian golf course architect and course shaper Riley Johns is an ardent fan of LivingStone and agrees that course has a unique presence, which he said most likely has to do with the fact that indigenous people inhabited the region for thousands and thousands of years.

"It has a character all its own. I attribute that back to it being sacred ground," Johns said. "There is a weird aura about the place and they did a really good job not disturbing that."

Johns, who is codesigner with Keith Rhebb of Winter Park, the 23rd-ranked nine-hole course in North America, discovered LivingStone while commuting to Mickelson National Golf Club, where he pushed dirt for Phil Mickelson's first marquee design in Canada. A sign on the TransCanada Highway alerted Johns to the existence of Living-Stone. Once he played, Johns knew he would be back.

"It's nine really neat holes," he said.

Being from the area, Johns knows the topography but still raves about the beauty of the golf course, which sits on the (east) prairie side of LivingStone Ridge, a sub-range of the Rocky Mountains.

He's enthralled with the old growth forest, the craggy gnarled and rare limber pines, some of which look dead but have been alive for hundreds of years if not more. In fact, the oldest known specimen in the world has been around for over 2,000 years. There are also the jagged ridges that Johns said remind him of the backs of Stegosauruses. Fissures run all through them.

"You can tell the landscape is alive," he said.

On the seventh hole at LivingStone Golf Course, players often pause to take in the view. The stand of trees on the left hides one of LivingStone's best-kept secrets. (*Riley Johns*)

The ridge is named after the famed African explorer David Livingstone, a Scot. It is an apropos name for the course, which Landry and Johns say can feel as if it were living.

What could be a magical round starts with a 413-yard, straightaway par-4 playing into the prevailing wind and nestled between two rock ridges.

The one on the left is covered in tall dense trees, while on the right clearing has occurred, so offline shots will find long grass.

The narrow feeling on the tee shot gives way to a more open hole from the landing area into the green. To the right of the putting surface is a mound, and the green tilts to the left with the back left corner falling off hard.

According to Landry, the first hole is indicative of the rest of the greens, plenty of subtle movement but "nothing extreme."

At 345 yards, the second hole is far less difficult than the first, although golfers are still going against the wind and playing between the two ridges but with an adequately wide fairway.

The long, narrow green is set much closer to the ridge on the left, but a gentle slope on that side will direct shots onto the carpet. To the right of the putting surface is a wide swath of dense rough and beyond that a narrow pond.

The green is the most benign at LivingStone.

"You make your money putting on that hole," Landry commented.

On the third hole, golfers for the first time get help from the wind that quarters off their right shoulders of this par-5 of 564 yards. From the back it requires a carry of 220 yards to reach the fairway. A true three-shot hole, the fairway rises gradually from about 115 yards into the green.

There is plenty of movement throughout the third as it bends gradually to the left.

According to Landry, the key to scoring here is to get close enough on the second shot so that a view of the green can be had on the approach.

For the second shot he recommends aiming for an immense boulder in the righthand rough, one of many such objects on the layout.

"The boys love their rocks," Landry said.

The putting surface is wider in the first half than the back and tilts back to front. A ridge running perpendicular to the line of play bisects the green.

At 417 yards, the fourth hole is another par-4, this one playing downwind.

Landry said from the elevated tee, the green that is slightly angled to the line of play resembles a pair of emerald lips.

With the fairway more open than on any of the previous holes, the fourth is defended by its putting surface. Players encounter a false front, while the back left falls off severely.

On the right, though, the green bends slightly around a mound that can guide poor shots back to the putting surface; it's this curve that gives the green its lips look.

Five is the first par-3 of the day, 177 yards and playing almost directly into the prevailing wind.

A series of tees is elevated and staggered; the front ones are the lowest and the rear set the highest, giving the option to play the hole from a variety of angles and distances.

The fairway leads into the mostly flat green that tilts a bit to the left and has, according to Landry, "a few subtle rolls and falls."

Except for the right side, there is plenty of room to miss the green without encountering much trouble.

Then there is the sixth hole, a doozy of a hole at a mere 262 yards that plays shorter due to a tail wind. This one is all about risk and reward. Sure, you can drive the green, which is blind from the tee and has a pond to the left, but there are a number of other possible results for the bold player.

"You can be out-of-bounds. You can be in the pond. You can lose a ball no problem," Landry said.

He advises hitting something like a midiron off the tee, since the second shot is downhill.

Johns raves about the hole. He said he knows he can use the land to run his tee shot onto the green, but a poor swing can put him in the pond or worse. The entertaining part begins once the drive disappears from view, since he has not a clue where the golf ball stopped.

"I'll have no idea until I get over the hill," John said.

Even before a club is swung on the seventh hole, it will imprint itself in the memory of all who play it as golfers encounter the finest view—a stunning vista—that LivingStone has to offer.

The tees are a hundred feet above the fairway, and from there players see the course, the massive rock ridges, and ranchlands. Turn around, and one can see the Rockies rise out of the plains.

A much-used bench sits near the back tee.

"Guys like to take a break and soak it all in," Landry said.

When golfers do step up, they are again faced with a risk-reward tee shot, this time on a 320-yard hole. The defining characteristic is a brook that runs across the fairway approximately 110 yards short of the middle of the green. Bombers that successfully carry the hazard can end up on the putting surface.

The fairway is slightly angled so the target from the tee is a large tree left and short of the green. The putting surface leans slightly right to left, so for those laying up staying left is best.

The back middle of the green has a hump-hollow tandem that makes putting in that area interesting.

The seventh also has a secret.

In the left tree line, almost directly across from where the cart path turns 90 degrees toward the fairway, is a natural spring of which even many regulars to LivingStone are unaware. Word is that is some of the best, if not *the* best, water on the planet. Stop and check it out for yourself before finishing the hole.

Then there is the eighth hole.

It is a par-3 that is almost all carry over marsh and pond to a green that is wider than it is deep, and slightly angled to the line of play. Here, though, is the kicker: from the back tees it plays 118 yards and from all the way up front, a mere 65 yards.

According to Landry, during last year's employee golf tournament, he put buckets of balls on the forward tees, and everyone was given two chances to *throw* a ball onto the green.

The right side of the putting surface has a slight Punchbowl rise to it, creating what Landry terms a "cauldron" design. Long and left is a safe place to miss.

Because of the size of the green, about 40 yards across, there will be some putts and chips of monstrous lengths. The putting surface tilts toward the water, but a good-sized strip of rough prevents balls from running into the drink.

LivingStone ends with another true three-shot par-5 that plays 534 yards from the back tees.

Immediately players will see that the fairway is two-tiered, with the right being higher. That is the preferred section. The two levels meld together about 75 yards from

A mere sand wedge for some players, from the back tee the eighth hole at LivingStone Golf Course plays all of 118 yards. (*Riley Johns*)

the green, and from there the fairway rises up to the putting surface enough so that an extra club is needed on the approach shot.

There is a mound on the front right corner of the large green and all the edges fall off, but the interior is mild with little movement.

Landry describes playing LivingStone as "a really fun round of golf," but golfers will also have the realization that "You've been challenged all the way through this golf course."

Johns lauds the Goodwins for forgoing sand hazards.

"You don't feel like you're missing bunkers," Johns said.

He attributes that to the fact that golfers are challenged in other ways, "by angles, blindness, and elevation."

According to Johns, LivingStone is attracting people from all over because it has no desire to be a country club, but rather a place where the average people can enjoy a great golf course, affordably.

"The unrefined aspect makes the course what it is," Johns said. "It's the place to go now."

BEYOND THE GREEN

There is nothing other than open space in close proximity to LivingStone, but Calgary is 30 miles to the east and the town of Cochrane 20 miles north.

Travel west for 50 miles or so, and you encounter the Rocky Mountains along with Banff National Park, Kootenay National Park, and Height of the Rockies Provincial Park, to name a few.

CHAPTER 16

Edgartown Golf Club, Edgartown, Mass.

Edgartown Golf Club is one of those rare layouts on which golfers of today encounter a course that has undergone few alterations since it opened over ninety years ago.

The original teeing grounds and greens appear to be exactly where they were in 1927, when golf balls were first struck on the layout.

The club was founded by Cornelius S. Lee, who paid $18,000 for the land upon which the club sits, formerly known as the Capt. Chase Pease Farm. The money collected from shares in the club was used to build the course.

Lee was the designer, and according to the club's website, "No architect was used and the only help he had was Bror Hogland, who was the first greens keeper. Bror said that the only help that he had was Cyrus Norton, leading the horse hired from Orin Norton while he ploughed the tees, fairways and greens."

The few modifications since 1927 have all been done in-house.

EGC is also one of those uncommon clubs that has stayed entirely devoted to golf. Not only are there no tennis courts or a swimming pool, but there is also no bar or restaurant. That does not mean the consumption of alcoholic beverages is forbidden or frowned upon. Rumor has it that a bottle can be easily found if there is a need to celebrate a stellar round or forget a lousy one.

Edgartown's first hole is not of the variety that welcomes golfers to the course with ease, whether they are playing to the lower green, or the newer higher green, which is

The vista from behind the small, domed sixth green with the seventh hole in the distance. (*Mark Hess*)

40 yards farther, above and to the right of the original putting surface. It is the only hole at EGC with two greens.

While the drive does not demand pinpoint accuracy, the approach sure does. There is a pond right of the green and a marsh short and left. A misplayed approach to either side results in an almost guaranteed double bogey to start the day.

The second hole is a wonderful par-5 that can be reached in two. As it should be, though, a pair of splendid shots is required to do so.

The tee shot is straightaway with a pond, a natural area, and scrub brush guarding the left, which is the preferred side if getting to the putting surface on the next shot is the desire. From here the hole bends left and rises perhaps 25 feet to the large green. Trouble continues down the left side, and a string of bunkers on the right guards much of the second landing area. Lies in this area are never level.

The miss on this green is short, as a row of small but steep mounds guards a good portion of the back. The defense of this putting surface comes in the way of small, almost invisible undulations throughout.

The third hole plays as a 299-yarder on the first go-round and a 157-yard one-shotter on the second.

As a par-4, tee balls encounter bunkers left and right of the landing area, but longer hitters will be able to get past them. A bunker short right of the green can come into play for those who suffered a poor effort with the driver.

A line of low mounds penalizes shots that run off the back of the green, and there is sand hazard to the left.

As a par-3, the tees are set well to the left of the fairway, almost on the property line. The left greenside bunker is very much a concern, especially when the flag is located on that side of the green.

The fourth hole can be challenged as a 402-yard par-4 or a 465-yarder with a par of 5.

Golfers turn into the prevailing wind for the first time, with the result being that the downhill hole plays much more difficult than the yardage would indicate.

Drives to the left side of the fairway on the dogleg left result in a better angle into the green and a shorter approach. A large bunker in the rough on the opposite side of the fairway captures those playing too cautiously off the tee.

The fairway narrows significantly short of the green. A bunker and two trees guard the left side, while a small pond is to the right and short of the putting surface, beyond which is found another tree and bunker.

The fifth hole is a delightful uphill par-4 of 299 yards that presents the player with difficulties from start to finish, not least of which is again playing into the ocean breeze.

From the rear markers, the distinct teeing ground is slightly below grade, and golfers must hit over two neatly trimmed hedgerows, which frame a dirt road that runs the length of the hole.

Again the left side is preferred, but to the left of the fairway is the aforementioned sandy way and beyond that out-of-bounds. Multiple bunkers once again guard the right.

From above the fifth green at Edgartown Golf Club, the view is across the course, Trapps Pond, Cow Bay, and out to the Oak Bluffs area of the island. (*Mark Hess*)

The approach shot plays uphill, and the elevation change will warrant at least a club more than the yardage.

Bunkers surround the green, and adding to the pressure of the approach shot is the fact that the clubhouse porch serves as a backdrop. On pleasant days there will be a gallery eyeing and assessing all who come through.

According to the scorecard, the sixth hole may look like a chance to catch one's breath playing 150 yards from the tips and 112 from the front, but one look at the green tells a different tale.

From the tees, it appears the green is flush against a stonewall on the other side of which is the road leading to the club. Two bunkers defend the front of the putting surface, while the left and right sides also have sand ready to catch imperfect shots.

Finally, finally, finally, the course flips 180 degrees, and the wind from the sea is now at the back of golfers for the par-4 seventh, the only hole that sits somewhat uncomfortably on the land. From tee to green, the elevation rises about 30 feet, but while the hole turns left to right, the slope of much of the fairway falls to the left.

Tee balls that land on the right of the fairway can carom down to the left, coming to rest in a relatively flat location, but leaving an uphill second shot to a green where only the flag is visible. Still, the green points to the left.

Shortening the hole by taking the line up the right side and approaching from the rough might not be a bad play, but there are two bunkers and a pair of trees that are a concern. Get past them, and the largest greenside bunker at EGC must be carried. Another bunker is behind the putting surface, and still another short left.

With a pond and an ocean serving as a backdrop, the eighth is Edgartown's most scenic hole, a true beauty. It might also be its most beguiling.

Playing with the wind and downhill, eight is a mere 285 yards, and therefore drivable, but to do so a number of perils must be avoided.

In the left rough, six yards from the center of the green is a bunker. Across the way in the right rough is another larger bunker and two trees. At the green, two sand pits guard the left and right corners with a third positioned back left.

In a stroke of downright brilliance by the designer, the green runs away from the line of play. The only buffer between the green and the watery confine of Trapps Pond is a narrow strip of rough through which a golf ball can seamlessly run. Big numbers can easily be made here.

Edgartown concludes with its finest hole, nothing short of great golf architecture from commencement to conclusion.

The 379-yard hole is into the wind and uphill to start. The fairway has internal movement neither seen nor felt anywhere else on the course; the green complex is diabolical.

At approximately 190 yards from the tee, the fairway gradually descends to low area perfectly guarded by a bunker in the right rough. Further ahead, there is another in the left rough that is unseen from the tee.

The saddle is the location from which to play the next shot but is significantly narrower than the rest of the fairway. Finding this spot is a bonus.

From here the hole is once again significantly uphill and still into the prevailing breeze. The shot to the putting surface is a tester.

Approximately 25 yards short of the green, the fairway again drops before rising drastically to the putting surface. An up-and-down from the swale before the putting surface takes skilled hands. The green is of comparable size to others at EGC, but the pinnable area is much smaller. The front third of the putting area is a false front, tilting back toward the low-lying approach.

All the rest of the way around, the edges of the green cause sharp drops that lead golf balls into the rough, or in the case of the back corner, to a bunker.

After the final putt is holed, hands shaken, backs slapped, and words of encouragement and congratulations exchanged, stop for a moment and absorb the view from the green. It will be difficult not to smile and whisper a thanks to the gods of golf.

Beyond the Green

There is an abundance of activities on Martha's Vineyard, from shopping to fishing, to whale watching, to even more golf. Besides Edgartown GC, there is the semiprivate Farm Neck Country Club, where former presidents Bill Clinton and Barack Obama often teed it up while in office. Mink Meadows is a 9-hole semi-private club designed by the team of Wayne Stiles and John Van Kleek.

Then there is the Royal and Ancient Chappaquiddick Links, a nine-hole 1,325-yard delight on the island of Chappaquiddick, literally a four-minute ferry ride from Edgartown. The course was founded in 1887 by the great-grandfather of the man who now single-handedly runs the place. The tiny greens, approaches, and minuscule tees are irrigated; the rest of the layout is not. The turf of the fairways and rough is whatever is indigenous to that part of the world. The course is an absolute delight to play, tailor-made for hickory clubs. Royal Chappy regulations require that all golfers play while wearing clothes. Sandals, cutoffs, bikinis, and flowing dresses are acceptable.

CHAPTER 17

Allandale Golf Course, Innisfil, ON, Canada

Brian McCann has spent nearly his whole life at the Allandale Golf Course. It was his home layout growing up in Innisfil, Ontario. In 1969, at the age of twenty-five, McCann purchased the lease of the course, a year after marrying, and has been running the facility ever since. He is now seventy-four.

It is truly a family affair behind the counter and on the mowers at Allandale. Brian's wife Marg is employed at the course. Their two children grew up there, learning to love the game. Daughter Michelle is an accomplished amateur golfer who also works at the facility in varying aspects. Their son John is a PGA of Canada professional who operates two driving ranges in the area. He spent time on the Canadian Tour and the Tour de Los Americas in South America. All three of Michelle's children, Lauren, Brendan, and Cole, pitched in at Allandale.

John holds the course record of 30, outdoing his father's best round by two shots.

Allandale is a Stanley Thompson design that began as a six-hole layout in about 1932. It was built for Donald and Marg Hogarth as part of their Mardon estate. Approximately three years later, Thompson returned to add three more holes, and the layout has remained virtually unaltered since then.

"We kept everything as is," said Marg. "If a tree came down, my husband put up a new tree."

At the point in his career when he designed Mardon, Thompson had the young American Robert Trent Jones as his partner. Jones would go out on his own a few years later and become the most prolific golf course architect on the planet in the post-Second World War era.

Keeping faithful to Thompson's work has caught the attention of Thompson fans, many of whom make it a priority to visit Allandale.

Stanley Thompson Society member and Thompson historian Dr. James M. Harris penned this about the nine-hole layout that will appear in his forthcoming book on Thompson:

"My experience at Allandale was that it is truly rustic in the best sense and it is like a journey back in time, small gravel parking lot, shack like pro-shop, mom and pop operators, yet great golf holes and a pleasure to play."

Canadian golf course architect Ian Andrews echoed the point in his Caddyshack blog.

"Allandale is all there, still intact, like stepping back [in time]," he wrote.

The layout is located about 45 miles north of Toronto. Donald Hogarth was a wealthy mining financier and a member of Legislative Assembly of Ontario. Combining "Marg" and "Don" resulted in the Mardon name. Their massive summer home, formerly Mardon Lodge, is now the Kempenfelt Conference Centre located on the shore of Lake Simcoe, a short walk to the golf course. Donald Mackenzie Waters, who was one of the architects who collaborated on Maple Leaf Gardens, designed Mardon.

The original routing was 7-9, 1-2, and 6 of today's course, starting and ending on a par-3. When the three holes were added, the layout also began on the current seven and finished on six. When the clubhouse was moved after the sale of the property, the fourth hole turned into no. 1, resulting in Allandale becoming one of the only Thompson designs with consecutive par-3s.

After Hogarth died, the course was sold to Harvey and Lola Foster in 1951. They renamed the course after their son, Allan. In 1968 the Ontario government purchased

Well-known pictorial map artist Ruth Taylor White created this whimsical drawing of the Allandale Golf Course, then known as Mardon Lodge, in about 1935. White was friends with the owners of Mardon, Marg and Donald Hogarth. White did not portray anyone playing golf, but there is plenty of (odd) activity going on outside the course. (*Courtesy of Richard Hogarth*)

Not every round at Allandale begins with a rainbow, but every round starts with a testing Stanley Thompson-designed par-5. (*Allandale Golf Course*)

the entire Mardon Lodge property, and a year later Brian McCann took over running the golf course.

It appears that from the outset Allandale was a tree-lined layout. An aerial photograph that could have been taken as early as the late-1930s and as late as the mid-1950s shows a portion of the course, and trees are a dominant feature, a rarity for designs of that time. A painting of the course from the late-1930s indicates the same. Perhaps the Hogarths were straight-ball hitters and used the narrowness to their advantage in matches against friends.

Green sizes are smaller than what is usually found on Thompson layouts. Brian McCann, who is also the course superintendent, said their dimensions average about 4,000 square feet, but some are much smaller.

Thompson's design has a trio of par-5s, par-4s, and par-3s. It plays to a par of 35 and is 3,025 yards from the back tees.

Allandale gets going with a straightaway par-5 of 500 yards. About 350 yards off the tee are two grass bunkers, filled with sand when the layout opened, bisecting the fairway, a hazard that will grab the attention of the golfer who has played a poor tee ball and looks to carry them on the next shot.

The front half of the putting surface is flat, but the latter portion tilts back to front. Thompson's signature mounds are found at the back of the green and partially along the right side, all waiting to inflict just desserts on errant shots.

A pair of bunkers guard the green short and wide left as well as short and wide to the right. The one short right will grab a first-timer's attention, as it is oval in shape with a narrow strip of sand surrounding a grass island. It's not the last of that style that players will encounter at Allandale.

At 375 yards, straight and without a bunker, the second hole might appear to be a cakewalk, but Thompson incorporated plenty of intrigue here.

The fairway is one of the more open at Allandale, sitting above the surrounding terrain while leaning a bit left to right. A tee ball too far right can catch that slope and end up somewhere on the third hole, an awful location from which to play the ensuing shot.

Then, farther up on the left, perhaps 15 yards or so short of the putting surface and continuing past it, there is a steep drop-off that will usher shots well into the rough. The green, of course, leans right to left so that poor approach shots that run off that side will continue on until ending in an unhappy location.

There is a bit of mounding behind the putting surface.

The third begins a trio of holes added a few years after the first six were played. It is a par-3 of 180 yards that ends at a tiny putting surface.

Golfers play out of a tree-lined corridor to a green that has a bunker back left and grass bunker right. According to McCann, the putting surface was originally guarded in front by a pond. When and why it was filled in is unknown.

McCann noted that the third hole is indicative of all the putting surfaces at Allandale.

"Every green is fun to put," he said. "They have subtle breaks you don't see."

One hole that is significantly different from the original design is the fourth, a four par of 375 yards that curls easily from left to right.

A feeling of openness is evident from the tee. According to McCann, a large stand of elm trees down the right side was lost a number of years ago to disease. One tree on the right side at the start of the fairway and two more at about 235 yards are enough to convince many golfers to play out to the left.

The green is raised above the fairway and is a tricky one to hold, according to McCann. Shots that land short of the putting surface will stop and those that come down at the midpoint or beyond without exception run off the back and don't stop rolling until they get to the fifth tee.

"The hole appears easy," McCann said but guarantees it is not.

Five is a par-5 that increases in difficulty the closer the player gets to the green, and it features one of Thompson's more artistic bunkers. It is also McCann's favorite hole.

At 490 yards, it begins with an undemanding tee shot. Trees lean in from the right side, but the left is open and the first 250 yards is straight.

From there the hole turns slightly to the left, and from about 70 yards in the fairway rises sharply. The players electing to go for the green in two will have a view of the flagstick. Those laying up will most likely have to use an aiming pole behind the putting surface as a reference for the approach shot.

Seventy yards from the green is an ideal location from which to play a third shot, so in the left rough Thompson placed an elaborate bunker to detain golf balls that missed the fairway. The thin strip of sand wraps around a mound of turf looking like the tail of a capital J, Y, or Z in looped cursive penmanship. The soil that was removed to create the bunker was mounded on the green side of the hazard, making a shot from the sand to the putting surface exceedingly difficult.

The green may appear to be flat but in reality tips from right to left. A large bunker runs the length of the green on the left, and on the right another bunker with a grass island is situated. Behind the putting surface, Thompson placed mounding.

Six is one tight par-3, but judging from the old aerial photograph of Allandale, it has always been that way.

The 155-yard hole sits on a flat piece of ground. Three bunkers just visible from the tee are at the putting surface, one well short and left, another at the left front corner, and the third across the way at the right front corner. Golfers, though, must also deal with a large maple that hangs over the right side of the green.

Mounds at the back of the putting surface hold back shots played too far, preventing them from finding out-of-bounds.

Seven is a par-3 as well and has slightly more room than the sixth. The original first hole is 210 yards and has the most undulations of any putting surface on the course.

The sixth hole is a tight, tree-lined par-3 that apparently is exactly as it was when the course opened. (*Allandale Golf Course*)

Three sand hazards also guard this one-shotter. Off the front left is a pot bunker and next to it a large tree that appears to already be mature in the early photo of Allandale.

To the right of the green, a bunker runs the length of the carpet. The pit is set between two large mounds, one behind it and one between sand and short grass. On the left a bunker also runs the length of the green.

Here the putting surface movement is prominent. The center area is a bowl. Beyond the depression, the wings on either side fall off to the green surrounds.

It is on the seventh hole that McCann witnessed one of his more memorable moments at Allandale. The legendary Canadian golfer, Moe Norman, considered to be one of the game's all-time best ball strikers, frequently played Allandale when his nearby home course of Branford Country Club was hosting an event. Norman was an unusual person with a quirky character and a unique golf swing that he devised on his own. Tiger Woods was quoted as saying only two players in the history of golf owned their swing, Moe Norman and Ben Hogan.

"You had to let him play two balls. He was an odd duck," McCann said chuckling at the recollection of Norman at Allandale. "I could have played golf with him a lot, but I didn't."

One time McCann was working on the tee of the seventh when Norman came to the tee of the sixth.

McCann turned and watched as Norman's first shot landed and stopped what McCann estimates to be two feet right of the hole. The second shot followed, and when it came to a halt it was two feet left of the cup, almost as if Norman did it intentionally. McCann was left shaking his head.

Another time McCann asked Norman what his best rounds were, and Norman snapped back his answer in the form of question: in competition or messing around?

McCann replied, both.

Norman said he shot a 57 at Branford and a 59 in a Canadian pro event.

Norman's best round at Allandale is unknown; he never discussed his score.

When golfers play the eighth hole, they will encounter topography they have not experienced at Allandale. The 380-yard hole starts at an elevated tee and pitches down to about the 200-yard mark, then changes direction and rises the rest of the way to the green. The fairway, however, is replete with rolls, humps, and pockets unlike any other on the course. It appears Thompson just used what was there.

"You look at it and you don't quite believe it," McCann said. "It's just the lay of the land."

The tee shot is tight with trees squeezing from both sides. The fairway then opens up, but the nearer to the putting surface one gets, the more the trees come back into play.

According to McCann, the green is deceptive, appearing nearly flat, but in reality it has a significant fall from back to front. Two bunkers, one on each side, flank the putting surface.

At the back, Thompson positioned mounding closer to the carpet than any other place at Allandale. McCann said he barely had enough room to cut a collar. As a result, a golf ball that rolls too far invariably means a subsequent shot with at least one foot on the mound and sometimes two, creating an awkward stance.

Just as it began, Allandale ends with a par-5. This is the only hole on the layout where McCann made a substantial modification to the design he found.

The ninth hole plays 525 yards. Trees are on both sides, gradually constricting the fairway until the hole corridor is all of 30 yards wide at the green.

McCann likens the tee shot to the 18th at Augusta National Golf Club, with the golf ball emerging from a tall chute of trees.

The fairway rises from beginning to end totaling some 20 feet and melds into a long, narrow green. McCann said he was forced to expand the original small putting surface because it did not hold up to a season's worth of traffic—unsurprising considering the layout was built for a wealthy couple and their friends, not as a daily fee layout.

Two large bunkers are on the right side of the putting surface, and there's also a much smaller one on the left. The entire rear of the green is backstopped by a large wrap-around sand hazard. Small humps on the edges accentuate the pits.

There is another factor that golfers have to deal with at nine, beyond the trees and bunkers—the first tee is immediately to the right of the green, and just past that the small clubhouse where those who are gathered observe the play.

"There's a lot of people watching the ninth," McCann said.

Beyond the Green

Innisfil, with a population of approximately 31,000 and a summer seasonal population of an additional 4,000, is a warm-weather destination. The Cookstown neighborhood is renowned for its antique stores and also hosts an annual "Wing Ding," which includes community yard sales, music, and food.

Alcona has Summerfest and a love for visitors. "Tourists? We've got 'em. We love 'em. Enjoy your visit!" reads the Alcona website.

Nearby is Sunset Speedway, a NASCAR-sanctioned facility that most often hosts races featuring Late Models, Super Stocks, and Mini Stocks. Also not far is Georgian Downs, which is home to harness racing.

CHAPTER 18

Norfolk Golf Club, Westwood, Mass.

Something doesn't add up about the history of Norfolk Golf Club.

If the history is to be believed, then sometime in about 1896 six members of the newly-formed NGC walked the nearly 44 acres of land known as the Wetherbee Farm and laid out a golf course, which, except for the slight relocation of one green, has stayed identical since.

Here's the problem—Norfolk, located in Westwood, Massachusetts, approximately 25 miles south southeast of Boston, is too good to be designed by a half dozen men whose names are long lost and who ostensibly knew nothing about design. What they devised is a challenging, enjoyable 2,968-yard course with a bevy of architecturally sound holes that could easily belong on a layout of a number of well-known architects. Just the fact that no two holes run in the same direction until the eighth and ninth seems to indicate those who designed Norfolk had more than an inkling about the craft:

Outing magazine touted the layout in May of 1899:

"The Norfolk Golf Club was organized in the spring of 1897, and a course of nine holes laid out near Islington station of the New England Railroad. Most of it was old pastureland, on which the turf was close and hard, requiring little to be done on the fair green. There are ponds and, of course, stonewalls but these may be made into useful hazards. The links run over a picturesque country, with a splendid view of the lowlands in the distance."

Golf was such an unknown game when Norfolk opened that it led to confusion among nongolfers, according to one publication from the day:

"The Norfolk Golf Club of Dedham, Massachusetts, scheduled one of its Saturday tournaments as a 'single-stick match.' This is a case in which the use of the word stick for club landed a committee in a position where it had to explain that golf was the game to be played, and that there would not be an exhibition of fencing on the day in question."

The putting surface on the eighth hole at Norfolk has a variety of features that will affect the roll of the golf ball. There is a false front, a mini Punchbowl, and flat sides, while the back leans away from the line of play. (*Jon Zolkowski*)

Overall, the layout of NGC has stayed nearly the same since at least the mid-1920s. Only the fourth green was moved slightly right of its original location, and that was to make room for a town road expansion. A 1927 scorecard lists the distance of the layout as 2,954 yards, 14 yards shorter than the current length.

There has been much bunkering added to the layout since the 1950s; some enhance the design, while others, unfortunately, take away the bump-and-run option. One of the worst bunkers in the history of modern golf course design was added somewhere in the 1980s and removed in 2000 by a superintendent who should have a plaque on the wall of the clubhouse honoring his good sense.

With the first hole at NGC, you know you are onto something special. The dogleg left of 405 yards begins with a downhill tee shot. Carry the bunker carved into the hill on the inside of the turn, and the approach shot is much shorter than playing it safe. The large green is perched on a shelf perhaps 30 feet above the fairway, atop a steep slope. Any approach that is short is not staying on the incline, and shots that run long will find bunkers that were added in recent years to prevent golf balls from making their way to the eighth tee.

This is a formidable way to begin the day.

The second is a snaking 384-yarder where again challenging a bunker on the inside of the left turn sets up the favored angle into the green. Bail out, and a huge bunker in the right rough just might have to be carried on the next shot.

The approach can be run onto the putting surface that has significant movement in it and requires skill with the putter to get the golf ball down in two.

The strong start continues with a testing short par-3 of 128 yards.

The third hole is 128 yards and slightly uphill, but three bunkers guard the front and slightly, perhaps too much, obscure the green, which tilts left to right severely enough that the flag location must be taken into consideration on the tee ball. This is not a hole on which one wants to be putting downhill or chipping downhill. Tree removal in recent years gives an expansive view from the tee out across the first fairway and takes away any real depth perception for the golfer, a wonderful bit of original strategy for such a short hole.

The par-4 fourth—really a 4 ½ for the average golfer—is an intriguing hole with lots of distractions that also rewards the long and straight player.

The fairway rises severely with the walkway from the parking lot crossing near the apex of the slope approximately 190 yards off the tee. Because of the hill, drives have a tendency to hit and stop, resulting in little carry off the tee and an awkward uphill lie for the second. Farther up on the right is the clubhouse, which is easily hit by an errant shot; the Plexiglass windows on that side of the building are proof positive.

The longer players who can get to the crest of the hill in one will find a large flat area and just 160 yards to the green that is at least 40 feet below the hilltop. It is the only domed putting surface at NGC.

The original green was positioned 30 yards left of its current location, almost abutting the out-of-bounds.

The fourth is also the site of tragedy.

In 1938, New York Giants starting left tackle Leonard "Fish" Grant was killed by a lightning strike while playing with three Norfolk members. Grant was vacationing and staying nearby at his parents' home when the incident occurred.

According to a *New York Times* article, raindrops fell and Grant wanted to stop, but the other three convinced him to continue.

"A second later the bolt struck, with an explosion that rocked the clubhouse twenty yards away," the story read.

The other three in the group, as well as a player on the nearby ninth green, were thrown to the ground but uninjured.

"Mr. Grant had been holding an iron club, and it was believed that the current coursed up the club to his arm."

Three doctors on the fifth fairway raced to his aid, "and the Dedham firemen worked vainly over the body with an inhalator for an hour."

Grant, who had starred at New York University and had just completed his eighth season with the Giants, was part of the 1934 team that won the NFL Championship.

Norfolk's fifth hole has no such dark tale in its history, but the 400-yard uphiller is another assignment for the average and shorter hitters. Length again is a massive

The tough uphill fifth hole at Norfolk Golf Club ends at a green that demands golfers fly their approach shot to the putting surface. (*Jon Zolkowski*)

advantage, not just because of the rise in elevation, but because the ground game was eliminated with the addition of bunkers in the last twenty years. Reaching the green is only done through the air.

Going long on the approach is not an option; all that is to be found off the back is serious trouble. The putting surface is one of the few that is severely banked from back to front.

The sixth is the kind of quirky hole that modern architects have a difficult time convincing their clients is worthy of being built. The way it is designed, a golfer who is accurate but short off the tee can achieve par as easily as the one who ends up long and straight.

It's 205 yards down the same hill the fifth hole climbed. Flying a shot to the green is an option, but landing the golf ball short—well short—of the putting surface and letting it run on is a wise choice, since just off the back of the putting surface is all kinds of nastiness that results in an atrocious lie or a lost shot.

Utilizing the ground off the tee harks back to the origins of Norfolk, when the golf ball was harder and the ground firmer.

A well-played shot that lands 165 yards from the tee can most certainly find the desired destination. It is a joy to behold, the white orb disappearing over the hill then reappearing as it finds its way onto the green that has a neat little swale on the right middle running perpendicular to the line of play.

The lone greenside bunker is on the right. At one time three well-placed diagonal cross-bunkers added to the hole's allure. Only the smallest one remains. It would be great to see the lost pair reinstated.

The only three-shotter on the course is the wonderfully maddening seventh, at 460 yards. The longest players should find the green in two, while all others should have nothing but a short- to midiron in hand for the third shot.

Here's the problem—the hole starts off bending right to left around a steep tree-covered hill on top of which is the eighth green. The dogleg appears more fearsome than it actually is because the left side of the hole is daunting. At the tee, trees are uncomfortably close, probably feeling more so because of the steep slope on the right. The hole opens up as it progresses, but as the trees on the left thin out they give way to out-of-bounds stakes and Downey Street after that. Oh, and there are two bunkers in the left rough just to make the hole corridor feel even more narrow.

From the first landing area, the fairway narrows and bends left as is also falls off toward the green, which appears to nearly touch the macadam of Downey.

At one point in the life of Norfolk, the putting surface could be accessed by the ground game, but no longer. Rough that extends 40 yards back from the green prevents that. A bunker flanks the left front and two others guard the right side. There is also sand back left. A shot played beyond the carpet finds woods.

The eighth could be classified as a drivable-undrivable par-4. It's an uphill hole that is all of 289 yards, but a large bunker in front of the green makes getting a tee shot to the hole all but impossible, save for a ridiculous bounce or two.

The rub, though, is that laying up is no simple matter. The fairway arches up so severely at one point that most shots, which land in a highly desirable location, bounce away and into the left or right rough.

The right is the preferred side as the left fairway falls severely off to a good 20 feet below the crown. From that location, the shot to the green is blind.

For good measure, there's also a bunker nestled into the ground below the fairway. From there, an uphill sand shot of 85 yards to an obscured putting surface is what is required.

For a while, the eighth hole was the site of an architectural travesty that bordered on a crime.

Somewhere in the 1980s or so, the club decided the bunker fronting the eighth green should be made into the shape of a giant, well-defined "X." It's as if Norfolk were trying to signal the occupants of the International Space Station.

The good news is that thanks to a former superintendent, the blunder was rectified, and a traditional-style bunker was reinstated.

Norfolk comes to an end with a par-3 that on a busy day can ratchet up the intensity, due to its location. It's a gentle downhill affair of 186 yards. There is a wide opening in front of the green that is flanked by a pair of bunkers, one right and one left.

The right and left sides of the putting surface fall toward the middle, which runs away from the line of play.

What can make the hole such a hellish undertaking is that there is usually a built-in crowd watching.

Behind the putting surface is the practice green, and to the left is the first tee, while back and to the right is a section of the clubhouse deck. On a busy day golf on the ninth is the center of attention.

The upside of the location is the satisfaction that comes with making a good score under the watchful and judging eyes of the assembled golfers.

BEYOND THE GREEN

Two highly acclaimed craft breweries are less than a 10-minute drive from Norfolk—Trillium Brewing Co. in Canton and Castle Island Brewing Co. in Norwood. They have been named to several national and local lists for top craft beer producers and would serve as perfect 19th holes.

If more golf is the choice, the Blue Hill Country Club is located in Canton. Designed by Donald Ross's personal caddie and protégé, Eugene "Skip" Wogan in 1925, the third 9 was added in the 1960s by Wogan's son, Phil.

Blue Hill hosted the 1956 PGA Championship won by Jackie Burke Jr., who also captured the Masters that year.

Through much of the 1990s, the LPGA Tour held an event there.

CHAPTER 19

Gibson Island Club, Gibson Island, Md.

In no way is it unfortunate that the course at the Gibson Island Club is one of North America's finest nines.

If the newspaper articles about the original layout, the plans, the few remaining photos, and the remnants of the course amidst the wood and backyards of the island are an indication, then the 18-hole layout Charles Blair Macdonald conceived and built there was a golf course to rival any in the United States and was possibly on par with his greatest creation, National Golf Links of America.

In a letter from Macdonald to W. Stuart Symington, Jr., the man behind the creation of Gibson Island, Macdonald wrote prior to the opening: "Gibson Island Golf Club has the finest course in the United States, a monument of which Baltimore and Maryland will have cause to be proud."

That same year Macdonald, according to a newspaper account, called Gibson the best course in the country during a dinner at Oakland Country Club on Long Island.

While designers then and now liberally throw around such undeserved compliments of their work, that was not Macdonald's way.

It was not just Macdonald touting the layout. Others were comparing Gibson to NGLA, Pine Valley, and The Country Club in Brookline, Massachusetts.

National was Macdonald's pride and joy. The holes were based on the finest ones in the world. Its construction was a labor of love. NGLA was his home course and his summerhouse overlooked the layout. Nothing he designed after it approached the greatness of National, except, it seems, for Gibson Island. Why he decided to eclipse National, at least in his own mind, is unknown. It wasn't about money. Macdonald designed for free and only for his friends, people like the Rockefellers and Vanderbilts.

It appears, too, that Gibson was the only project on which Macdonald laid out 36 holes, although only 18 were built. His protégé and chief course builder, Seth Raynor, who was a phenomenal course architect in his own right, drew up 36 on a few occasions, but not Macdonald.

The surviving Gibson Island plans found at the Frederick Law Olmstead National Historic Site show both courses drawn onto a map that includes hundreds of home lots. Olmstead and Sons, the landscape architect for the project, was the preeminent firm in their field.

The life span for the majority of the first 18 was stunningly short, especially considering the phenomenal quality of the golf course. Many of the holes had views of the Chesapeake Bay with the five most scenic holes running out and back on a narrow peninsula that stretched into the Magothy River.

On some of the ground the course once occupied, there are homes, but portions of the former layout have reverted to woods and are located on protected land, former greensites easily located.

On the Gibson Island nine of today, holes 1-2, 4-5, and 7-9 are complete or portions of what Macdonald originally designed there. The two par-3s, the third and sixth, are not his in any way, shape, or form.

Symington's goal in creating Gibson Island, dubbed "the Newport of the South," was to make the island a summer and weekend retreat for the wealthy in the Washington D.C.-Baltimore, Md. area. In 1921, he hired Macdonald, considered the father of golf course architecture in the US.

In his entire career, Macdonald laid out fewer than 15 courses including the Piping Rock Club on Long Island, St. Louis Country Club, and the Mid-Ocean Club in Bermuda.

How Symington convinced Macdonald to accept the project remains a mystery. Macdonald was a prominent member of the New York Stock Exchange, and the two may have known each other through friends or business dealings.

Construction on the Gibson course began in 1922, and the first nine opened for play a year later. On Memorial Day Weekend of 1924, the entire 18 was playable, and the club hosted an inaugural three-day invitational featuring a small field of nationally and regionally known amateurs and professionals. Before the grand opening, the course received a detailed review in the *Baltimore Sun* newspaper, which feted the Macdonald design in glowing terms and included photographs.

Then, just six weeks later, Symington and his new greenkeeper, Scotsman William S. Lindsay, started significantly altering the layout.

"At least 10 of the 18 holes at the course at Gibson Island will come in for changes of a more or less radical nature," read a *Sun* story.

The problem, it seems, was that the design was too difficult.

"Determined to bring about the speediest possible realization of his original resolve to produce a golf course equally suited to the dub, the average player and the champion, W. Stuart Symington, Jr., has actively embarked on a campaign of thorough renovation and radical alteration at Gibson Island," read the *Sun*.

The article went on to say the layout "provides too exacting a test even for the champion. For the dub or average player it is well-nigh prohibitive."

Symington, it was reported, consulted with Jess Sweeter, winner of the 1922 U.S. Amateur and who had captured the Gibson Island event, as well as local amateurs and club professionals.

According to the piece, Symington also talked with "Charles Raynor," which might be an accidental coupling of Charles Macdonald and Seth Raynor.

Every move by Symington detailed in the newspaper account radically altered a hole, as tees and fairways were shifted, marshes and bogs filled in, and the contours in greens softened.

"Cavernous traps with their deep, perpendicular wall will be modified so that it at least will be possible to get out with the loss of a reasonable number of strokes. This

Perched high above its surroundings, the first green at the Gibson Island Club was part of the original Charles Blair Macdonald 18-hole design and has views of the Magothy River and the Chesapeake Bay. (*Don Skacan*)

means the slopes next to the green must be graded and grassed in some instances," reported the *Sun*.

More alterations occurred than what was detailed in the article. For instance, the 18th green was moved 110 yards toward the tee and to its current location. The remaining original greens lack the style described in the article.

"Many of them are irregular in shape, this irregularity being so conformed to the fairway as to call for additional skill in approach shots" is how the originals were described in the *Sun* preview article.

It appears that by 1929 the layout had been shortened to nine holes, possibly for financial reasons, although the club was active and even hosted an annual women's golf tournament starting in 1927. A May 1929 article said real estate sales were up due to the recent addition of a concrete highway and that an electric line would soon be extended to the island.

Yet, with all the confounding changes and the loss of a majority of the original holes, what remains at Gibson Island is a set of nine that is among the best there is.

Strategy is still there, shot making, is required, and the incredible boldness bordering on lunacy that Macdonald incorporated into his layouts is easily identifiable.

Gibson can stretch to 3,176 yards and a par of 36.

The layout opens with a hole 415 yards that is a bear in its length but lets the golfer err thanks to a hole corridor that is 80 yards wide at points. Two fairway bunkers on the right should not come into play.

The tee shot is down and the approach plays up, about two clubs' worth of climb. The green, with bunkers on both sides and in the back, is angled and leans away from the line of play. Long approach shots can be run onto the putting surface.

The second at 410 yards is the opposite of the opener. The fairway rises up from the tee and descends to the green. A bunker sits into the crown of the fairway on the left and is unlikely to be reached off the tee. It is, though, a visual distraction when an approach has to be played over it.

The green is tilted back to front, the most severe of that style on the course. A strip bunker on the right sits well beneath the putting surface, giving a hint of the penal style that was found on the layout when it opened.

The third is a nonoriginal hole of the Punchbowl style. It plays as far back as 185 yards. It is obviously not a Macdonald or Raynor design, too small to begin with. It is, though, fun with a tee shot over a finger of a pond as well as a steep bank in front of the green that sends miscues back into the water. The bowl feature performs as it should, reining in and redirecting poorer shots.

The fourth is classic Macdonald, even though it has been tamed somewhat. It plays shorter than the listed length of 360 yards because of the downhill fairway that also cants right to left. Taking the tee shot down the right, then, is the recommended play. For the longest hitters getting within a few yards of the green complex is a distinct possibility.

Intrigue was added to the right side in the form of a fairway bunker implemented by architect Brian Silva some years back during a restoration-renovation. At 255 off the tee, it is in play for the average golfer, who must avoid running into it, and the longer players, who need to fly the pit. Find the sand, and the ensuing shot is 95 yards downhill to the carpet.

Two narrow strip bunkers nearly encircle the putting surface. The most difficult approach is from the left side, where the uphill approach shot is over the bunker that lies well below the putting surface. Putting here is a delightful challenge with movement throughout the green.

The Olmstead drawing shows a huge bunker that started at the end of the fairway on the right, wound around the back of the green, and then extended at least 50 yards up the left side of the hole corridor.

The fifth is the only hole on the course that plays shorter than the original, which was listed as 425 yards on an early scorecard. Since then a road was added and the back tee was moved up 10 yards.

It is a straightaway affair with a par of 4, the green not visible from the tee. There is a fairway bunker at 300 yards.

The putting surface is guarded on both sides and the rear with a string of pearl necklace bunkers that are typical of Macdonald's style found on such layouts as the Morris County Club in New Jersey.

The 158-yard sixth is a nonoriginal hole. It is a good par-3, the elevated green fronted by a pair of bunkers. On the left, right, and long, steep falloffs penalize inaccurate shots. The putting surface is wider than it is deep, a design style more Devereux Emmet—a Macdonald-influenced architect—than Macdonald himself.

Then there is the seventh that in all its glory gives a crystal clear vision of what Gibson Island once was.

It is a Volcano Hole that can be loved or loathed for its oddness. It was the 16th hole on the original course and 330 yards. The entire story of the hole, though, is told in the second shot.

The green must be one of the most peculiar Macdonald ever fashioned. It is oblong-shaped and sits diagonally to the fairway centerline, perched atop a severely sloped mound at least 20 feet above the low point of the fairway. The putting surface is 35 yards long but only 12 yards at the widest. Three narrow bunkers are cut into the hill

The eighth green at Gibson Island is a reverse Road Hole design. In the background is the ninth green. When the 18-hole course opened, golfers played to the left or over the hill that is some 60 yards short of the original green. (*Anthony Pioppi*)

well below the green surface. The slope leading up to the hilltop is of such severity that shots that land short of the target will run 30 yards back down to the fairway. Any golf ball off the back or sides that misses sand will tumble away 15 to 20 yards, at least.

What makes the seventh so confounding is that there is not a comfortable location from which to play the approach. The farther one is back from the green, the better the view of the putting surface, but a longer club is required to reach. The closer one gets to the upslope, the more the perspective of the green diminishes even though a shorter club is in hand.

Factor constant normal wind into the equation, never mind a blustery day, and the seventh surely must be one of the toughest short par-4s on the continent.

The eighth, another grand design, is far less intimidating and severe in its penalizing of poor shots but oozes Macdonald's bold style.

While the Great Design Triumvirate of Macdonald, Raynor, and Banks peppered their layouts with template hole designs modified for each site, only one remains at Gibson. The eighth is a Road Hole patterned after the 17th at the Old Course in St. Andrews, Scotland. With the Gibson version, the green is flipped so that the Road Hole Bunker is on the right and the best side from which to approach is the left.

The 17th hole of the original Gibson Island course, it plays 525 yards from the blue tees, the only par-5 on the card, and 410 yards and a par-4 from the gold tees, which might just be the preferred location.

From the back, the right fairway bunker that sits atop a mound—playing the part of the railway shed on the St. Andrews hole—is unreachable, but it is very much in play from the gold markers. The preferred line of play is over the bunker so the kick of the downslope can be taken advantage of. As a result, the hazard is an integral part of the strategy when the eighth is challenged as a par-4.

A bunker on the left of the fairway 110 yards from the green's center must be dealt with when the hole is played as a five, since that is the side to best approach.

Seventy-five percent of the large green is guarded by bunkers that, fitting with the overall scheme, are located a good distance beneath a putting surface that runs diagonally away from the line of play.

The strategy needed to successfully negotiate the eighth—and many others on the original 18—was accurately described the *Baltimore Sun* article previewing the opening:

". . . many of the holes are so laid out that the par-shooting golfer by boldly essaying certain natural hazards will have the chance to go from tee to green in two strokes while the less expert or less venturesome player can take the longer and safer way at the cost of one or two stokes."

The 382-yard ninth hole is about two-thirds of the original eighteenth, and what remains looms over the golfer like the remnants of a once-great castle.

When the ninth was built, the hill on which the green is located was the Alps feature of the design. The hole was 364 yards from the existing ladies' tee, and the line of play skirted the right side of the massive mound. Then, the green was located roughly where the crushed stone area is to the right of today's clubhouse.

Now, the hole plays 382 yards, and the fairway rises up gradually until it comes to the base of a massive hill. The better angle in is from the right side, so long a diagonal bunker 200 yards from the tee that's part of the original design must be carried if that plan is to be accomplished.

Perched atop the hillock, which once served to thwart approach shots to the original putting surface, is the green with strip bunkers around three sides. The front is the only open area.

When the round is over, it will be difficult not to pause and soak in the view—a wonderful way to conclude a round at Gibson Island.

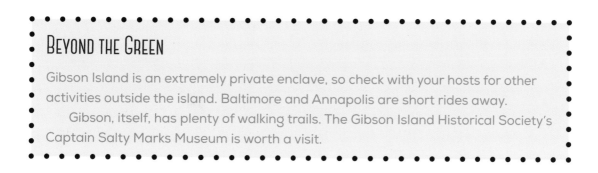

BEYOND THE GREEN

Gibson Island is an extremely private enclave, so check with your hosts for other activities outside the island. Baltimore and Annapolis are short rides away.

Gibson, itself, has plenty of walking trails. The Gibson Island Historical Society's Captain Salty Marks Museum is worth a visit.

CHAPTER 20

Kahuku Golf Course, Kahuku, HI

It's safe to say that when PGA Tour player Zac Blair is in town for an event, he would be welcome at nearly all the courses in the state.

An avowed fan of Golden Era golf course architecture, Blair likes to seek out the best area layouts and tee it up early in the week of the tournament.

So it speaks volumes that when Blair travels to Oahu, Hawaii, for the Sony Open, he bypasses the better-known facilities and heads over to the municipal Kahuku Golf Course with family and friends.

It plays 2,699 yards with a par of 35 and absolutely stunning ocean views on one side and mountains on the other. There are four par-3s, three par-5s, and a pair of par-4s. The turf has two heights of cut, greens and the rest.

"The old ironwood trees here have been bent by the wind, wildflowers bloom in the rough, and a thick growth of ice plant covers The Dunes Club" is how writer Grady Timmons described the setting in a 2002 newspaper article.

The story goes that in 1937 men working in the sugarcane fields of the Kahuku Plantation created the course. It has undergone a series of renovations since then, and whoever oversaw the design of the current course knew what they were doing. There is no architect's name attached to the original work or the subsequent renovations.

Yet, at Kahuku there is an abundance of variation in the holes and challenging greens. As a result, the course challenges golfers to employ significant strategy. Kahuku's designers had to be somewhat knowledgeable in architecture.

"It can't be a coincidence that there are so many good holes and so well thought out," Blair said.

The city operated the course under a lease agreement from 1952 until 2016, when the city and county of Honolulu bought 114 acres of oceanfront land for $12.1 million, including the course. Luxury homes were slated to be built on the site. About 25,000 rounds of golf are played at the course each year.

Since 1935, the layout has taken more than its share of abuse.

In February of that year, all began well when bunkers were added and fairways rebuilt with the help of local sportswriters who were enlisted for the project that was expected to take one day. They were invited to play in a tournament before the one-day renovation in order to "inspect" the layout.

Then barely seven months later, on Labor Day 1938, their toiling was effectively destroyed when the plantation hosted a massive rodeo at the course. According to reports, 15,000 people and 3,000 automobiles showed up.

A *Honolulu Advertiser* article described the day:

"There were horse races, roping events, plenty of exhibitions by the Army and a parade which expert observers of such things claim was one of the most colorful in Oahu history when gaily garbed pa'u riders, hula troupes and bands drew round after round of applause from an enthusiastic crowd that stretched far and away down the improvised race course over which the best island mounts thundered to cheers of thousands."

Prior to the event, one newspaper scribe had little hope for the layout surviving the onslaught.

"If there is anything left of the greens and tees after the celebration is over, then luck is with the golfers," he wrote.

Then on December 7, 1941, during the bombing of Pearl Harbor, an American B-17 bomber so shot up that, according to one account "It looked like a piece of Swiss cheese," made an emergency landing on a Kahuku fairway. The crew emerged unscathed. A few days later the plane was taken apart and trailered off the site. Then the course was plowed up to prevent Japanese planes from landing in an anticipated second attack.

Shortly after that the layout was used to house 5,000 troops for a few days, including Hawaii's first draftees.

Prior to and after the Second World War, the Kahuku fairways oddly became landing strips for groups of planes that were hopping around Oahu.

According to a 1950 newspaper article, planes participating in a "Breakfast Flight" used Kahuku as one of their stops. The pilots and guests of the first three planes from Oahu that landed there, as well as the occupants of the first two planes from other islands, received a free meal from Irei (the course restaurant).

The bad streak ended for Kahuku when the city took over running the course in 1952. The layout was closed for a few months as it underwent substantial renovation, reopening on July 4. By December of that year, Ernie Werner and his staff were commended for transforming the course into first-class condition.

An advertisement that ran in the 1938 *Honolulu Star-Bulletin* for the rodeo that was held on the Kahuku Golf Course and in likelihood decimated the layout. An estimated 15,000 people attended. (*Honolulu Star-Advertiser*)

Kahuku was almost lost in the mid-1980s when the Campbell Estate, which was then owners of the land, wanted the Kahuku site for sand mining and offered to give the city enough land across the road, on the mountain side, to build eighteen new holes. The proposal was rejected.

There was also a movement by the city about that time to expand Kahuku to eighteen holes, but that never came close to happening.

At first glance, Kahuku appears scruffy, almost ragged. Blair says not to be fooled. "It plays better than it looks," he said.

Blair was introduced to the course while playing for Brigham Young University's golf team. Every year the team participated in a tournament at Turtle Bay Country Club and it would visit Kahuku, almost as a lark, but Blair saw something special right away.

This ramshackle structure serves as the clubhouse for Kahuku, ironically giving no indication of the quality golf course that lies beyond. (*Honolulu Star-Advertiser*)

"I was the only one who thought, 'holy cow, this is really good,'" he said. "People don't know how good this is."

Part of what Blair admires is that Kahuku is kept firm so the ground game is a viable option to negotiate the layout and mitigate ocean winds. The fairways are only irrigated when Mother Nature sees fit to make it rain.

Kahuku begins with a 164-yard, downhill par-3. It is not viewed as an easy hole, and neither are any others on the course, because of the constant winds of 20 mph or more blowing off the nearby Pacific. The hole plays dead into the breeze.

There is a bunker to the left and bushes beyond the green, but short and right are safe places to miss.

The first par-5 of the day is the second hole, and it measures 457 yards, increasing in difficulty the closer players get to the green.

There is ample acreage off the tee with the sixth fairway adjoining to the left, so a centerline bunker 200 yards out and a series of grassy mounds 50 yards farther on can be easily avoided.

The hole narrows from the second shot and culminates at a green that is placed precariously close to an out-of-bounds fence on the right, which separates the layout from a cemetery.

With the winds coming off the ocean and left to right, playing away from the gravestones makes sense, but that leaves a pitch over a greenside bunker to a putting surface that runs from back right to front left.

The second of the one-shot holes is the uphill third, which makes it acutely clear that those involved with Kahuku's design knew what they were doing.

The length on the card is 149 yards, but the third hole is severely uphill with the prevailing wind quartering from the left. A few scrubby wind-blown trees behind the putting surface don't aid with depth perception. The infinite background is blue sky and high white clouds.

The two-tier green is marvelous. The right portion is larger and a good two feet higher than the left. Miss to that side, and shots bound away toward the ocean and into the thicket.

Tee shots landing right of the putting surface can roll away a good 50 yards.

There is, however, a bit of forgiveness. A slope behind a portion of the putting surface has punchbowl qualities and can guide long shots back onto the green.

From there, a short walk brings golfers to the tee of the fourth hole, another par-3 that is the complete opposite of the previous hole. It is 110 yards, plays severely downhill, and is always downwind.

The green is guarded in front by a large coffin bunker with a high lip.

"People have been whacking sand on it for years and it's built up," Blair said.

The putting surface is flanked left and right by two other bunkers. Going slightly long here finds no trouble.

A spine on a portion of the green makes for some entertaining putts.

According to the card, the fifth hole is exactly 200 yards longer than the fourth, a total of 310 yards.

Blair is effusive in his praise.

"This could be one of my favorite par-4s in the whole world," he said.

There is only one bunker on the hole, and it is right of the green.

The tee is nearly abutting the out-of-bounds on the left. The slightly rising fairway, which tilts right to left, is plenty wide for the players that pull driver, including those looking to reach the green from the tee.

The defense of the fifth hole comes by way of a two-level hourglass-shaped green with the back tier significantly higher than the front. Ending up right of the putting surface is acceptable; going left results in misery, as Blair knows firsthand.

"I missed left the last two years in a row and had no chance to make par," he said chuckling. "This is as good a drive and pitch as I've ever seen."

The final par-3 on Kahuku is the uphill sixth hole that measures 119 yards, with the green out of view and only a portion of the flagstick visible. The hole points toward the sea, making the tee shot a difficult one.

"Flight it low into the wind," Blair advised.

"The green is great. It was placed by a guy who knew what he was doing," he added.

In 1936, Emma Dunn, who according to the newspaper account was the wife of the chief foreman of the plantation, made the first-ever ace at Kahuku at the sixth hole while playing with her husband and another couple.

The seventh hole is a monster par-5 at 557 yards with spectacular viewing of the nearby beach from the elevated back tee that borders the out-of-bounds on the right.

With the wind coming from the right, the daring play is to take it down that side and let the breeze move the tee shot over into the fairway. It is the best route to avoid the left fairway bunker. The problem in going too far right is the white out-of-bounds stakes that line the hole.

The par-5 seventh at Kahuku Golf Course is the longest of the nine holes. The layout borders Malaekahana Beach and Kahuku Beach with the shimmering blue waters of Keone'o'io Channel beyond. (*Honolulu Star-Advertiser*)

For the second shot, a smattering of bushes left and right is the only problem.

The green is another of the hourglass designs with a bunker on each side where the putting surface necks in. The back portion of the carpet is slightly elevated above the front.

Two sand roads define the par-4 eighth hole, which is 375 yards.

The pathways are access roads to the beach and are in constant use by vehicles and people. The result is a pair of what Blair calls "trench bunkers" running diagonally across the fairway and resembling bunkers from American courses in the early days of golf. "The big hitters can carry the first but you have to get a bounce to get past the second," he said.

Ending up between the two is also a possibility, a fortunate result.

That which, to that point, was a flat fairway rises abruptly from about 65 yards out from the green, which is blind. A white flagpole beyond is the aiming point.

The putting surface runs back left to front right, and the rear portion of the green is bisected by a small ridge.

Like any good reachable par-5, the ninth hole at Kahuku presents a legitimate chance to make a good score yet also exacts a heavy toll for miscues.

"It's a cool finisher, because you feel like you can make birdie going out," Blair said.

The hole is 474 yards with a fairway that canters left to right and rises slightly from tee to green. While it is extremely wide to begin with, 115 yards in the first landing area, the fairway narrows as it gets toward the green, and here is where the hole toughens up. The putting surface is very near out-of-bounds on the right, and with the wind blowing in from the left, a daring second shot that looks good leaving the club can ultimately end in the neighboring property, but even laying up does not leave a simple third shot. Two bunkers guard the left and right front portions of the putting surface that Blair says has qualities of the Road Hole Green at the Old Course in St. Andrews, Scotland. Going slightly beyond the putting surface is acceptable.

According to Blair, Kahuku is a must-play. With some improvements, he said, it would be in the upper reaches of the finest nines.

"If you go to Oahu to play golf, you have to go there. It's the best golf course on the island," he stated. "If someone put some money into this, it would be one of the best nine-holers in the world. It's that unbelievable."

Beyond the Green

You're in Hawaii. You probably have it covered.

CHAPTER 21

Nehoiden Golf Club, Wellesley, Mass.

The narrow road into Nehoiden Golf Club in Wellesley, Massachusetts, will take you across the ninth hole, past a crushed stone parking lot and a wooden archway, and in front of the first tee. Not long after you will come to the Nehoiden House, a simple and appropriate structure for such a facility, except that it has nothing to do with the course.

Now turn around and go back to the stone parking lot and the arch. That *is* Nehoiden, officially named Nehoiden Golf Club at Wellesley College. There is no clubhouse, practice area, cozy restaurant, or for that matter, structure with four walls. The arch is it. Scorecards and pencils are found at the first tee, and if a course employee is not there to greet you, one will be along in short order to electronically record your season pass, or usher interlopers off the layout.

The private facility is run by the all-women's college that counts Hillary Clinton, Katharine Lee Bates (who wrote the words to "America the Beautiful"), and astronaut Pamela Melroy as alums.

The course is a hybrid of two designs, part of which dates back to the beginnings of golf at Wellesley in the late 1890s. The other portion is the work of Wayne Stiles and John Van Kleek, the highly acclaimed Massachusetts-based design duo best known for another college layout, the Taconic Country Club owned by Williams College in northwestern Massachusetts.

In the late 1920s, Stiles and Van Kleek produced an eighteen-hole drawing for Wellesley to supplant the nine holes it had. The Stiles-Van Kleek routing used all of the land that the course then and now occupies, plus more. For reasons unknown, the new design was nixed, but Stiles and Van Kleek updated what was there. Much of their work remains with just a few adjustments made over the years.

The course begins with a par-5 hole that can stretch to 450 yards. For the longer hitter this is more appropriately a par-4. In any case, it is a fun way to begin the round.

The drive is simple with a wide fairway and a flat landing area. It is good to make a mental note before beginning regarding where the green is located, since the second shot is blind.

Now the hole gets demanding. The second shot is straight up a 50-foot rise that offers no clue as to where the green resides. Trees frame the fairway left and right and from about 85 yards in can make the hole feel a bit confined.

There is one shallow bunker 30 yards short and right of the greensite, which sits on the edge of a small gorge. The seventh's putting surface and entire eighth hole are visible from here.

The course now turns 180 degrees and plays straight down the hill that was just ascended. At that start of the fairway is a tree that has no business being there even though it can be easily carried on the drive. Why on Earth it is directly in line with the middle of the fairway is mind-boggling.

The second hole bends sharply left with two groves of trees guarding the inside of the dogleg on the 374-yard hole.

The green that once sat on the tee side of Fuller Brook was relocated sometime in the 1960s over the stream, a brilliant move that created a daunting and fun approach shot, even with a wedge in hand. Short is water, to the left is sand, to the right is trees, and long is either out-of-bounds or a bunker.

The third is 180 degrees opposite of the second and is the most mundane hole on the golf course. The 313-yarder has a wide fairway. Two bunkers guard the green to the left and right.

Players turn around again to play the 200-yard par-3. There is a bunker 30 yards short of the green on the right and one just off the left corner. Two bunkers flank the right side of the green and there is trouble long. It provides a formidable challenge.

Members of the Wellesley College student body taking part in a golf class sometime prior to 1925. The spot where they are standing is in the vicinity of the existing seventh tee. (*Wellesley College*)

Turn back once again, and from here it is an entirely different golf course, starting with the 366-yard fifth. The influence of Stiles and Van Kleek is palpable.

From the tee the flag is barely visible, rising from a shelf that is perhaps 30 feet above the fairway.

A prominent ridge runs diagonally across the fairway, which is tree-lined on the right.

The approach shot can be daunting, requiring probably two clubs more to successfully ascend the heights. At about 45 yards short of the green the fairway juts seemingly straight up, appearing almost vertical from a distance.

It is a taxing walk to the green, but what a sight greets the golfers. The large putting surface is literally carved out of a hill and leans back to front, the rear portion running into a severe slope covered in extremely long grass.

The green could be so much better visually and playability-wise with just a little work. If extended to its intended dimensions, the putting surface would be in the neighborhood of 10,000 square feet, with the front collar nearly at the edge of the precipitous drop. If the back wall that is now covered in knee-high grass were mowed up just two more feet from the bottom, a world-class punchbowl would be created, allowing players to be bold with their plays into the green knowing the rise could be used as it was surely designed, to redirect golf balls back to the green. Now the fear of an impossible lie or even a lost ball dissuades golfers from getting too aggressive.

There are three paths to take when going for the sixth green at Nehoiden Golf Club. The slightest mistake, however, can send a shot onto Washington Street that runs perilously close to the putting surface. (*Cary Collins*)

The putting surface is chock-full of deceptive nuances that direct golf balls in unforeseen directions, a pure delight.

From there it is onto the sixth, arguably one of the coolest, quirkiest golf holes in greater Boston, an area that has an abundance of fantastic designs.

A sign at the tee gives a unique warning. If Wellesley College students are taking part in a physical education class at the small building and putting green located far down the hole on the left side, then the sixth and seventh are closed and golfers must proceed to the eighth.

The structure is most likely on the site of the original clubhouse. When it first opened, Nehoiden began on the current seventh hole and ended on the current sixth hole.

From the tee, the sixth at 369 yards appears uneventful, almost benign. There is one bunker in the right rough, while the fairway widens out to the left, with a generous portion of rough on the side before the wood line is encountered.

Oh, but then the fun begins. For the first time in the round, the fairway has movement to it, the heaves and pockets creating all sorts of uneven lies and awkward stances.

The approach shot cannot be taken without a walk to see what lies in store. Sixty-five yards from the center of the green a bunker stretches across two-thirds of the fairway. Beyond it the ground drops sharply, tumbling approximately 20 feet before it levels out at the green, which is flanked left by a drop-off and rough and on the right by a rough-covered rise.

Immediately past the putting surface is a row of arborvitae, followed by a chain-link fence, a public sidewalk, and finally Washington Street. In other words, don't go long.

Now, though, that the first-time Nehoiden golfer knows what lies in waiting, back at the golf ball a decision must be made on how to get to the green, and there is no single right answer.

The bravest of plays and the one requiring the most skill is to fly the ball directly to the green, using the house across the street as an aiming point. The problem with this choice is the severe penalty inflicted on a shot that flies too far or a tad short. Landing just off the green on the downslope will send a golf ball caroming past the putting surface and into bushes or worse, the same with a shot that flies too far.

The second option, which also requires aiming at the home on the other side of Washington Street, is for the approach to just carry the cross bunker and bounce its way down the hill to the putting surface. This avenue of play also presents problems. Find the bunker, and the next shot is a precarious sand wedge to a target 30 feet below.

There is, however, a third way to go, specifically designed for shorter hitters, and it might be the most fun.

Left of the fairway bunker, a saddle was dug out, creating a half pipe of sorts running with the line of play. The golfer who deftly lands a shot in the depression will often find that the feature directed the golf ball down the hill and onto the green, even from a great distance.

The seventh is the shortest par-4 on the course, drivable for some, with an odd, fun green that has more internal movement than any other at Nehoiden.

The fairway is the same as the previous, with rolls, dips, and knobs from start to finish. The backyards of homes on Dover Road abut the fairway, so any shot too far left means reteeing.

The putting surface is oddly set back some 20 yards from a falloff, on the other side of which sits the first green. The seventh green feels out of place, as if it should be hugging the drop-off. Twenty yards beyond the putting surface is a bunker in the shape of a new moon that is on the edge of the gully. It is separated from the green by a swath of native area and, as a result, hardly ever sees a golf ball.

The delightful par-3 eighth is next at 148 yards. It is a simple style of artistic golf architecture that unfortunately so many modern designers don't recognize or don't value.

Short of the green a ridge bows in from the left, with two expertly located bunkers carved into the ridge, and partially obscures a portion of the putting surface. The green has a pronounced back-to-front fall, and any golf ball that parks above the flag will take a skilled touch with the putter to get down in two.

The ninth—a 500-yard par-5 with an abundance of strategy that gives golfers a legitimate chance to make birdie while also equitably penalizing mistakes—is no letdown.

The architect team of Wayne Stiles and John Van Kleek expertly used the natural terrain and bunkering to create a deceptive and testing par-3 of 148 yards. (*Cary Collins*)

The elevated tee affords golfers a view of the entire hole including a stream that runs between the first and second landing areas, the entrance road that also bisects the fairway in the second landing area, and the green that is perched 20 or so feet above the fairway.

This is the fourth time a brook is crossed in the round, demonstrating the thought-fulness of the routing. Twice players cross the water on the tee shot, once on the approach shot, and here on the second shot of a par-5 where the sliver of a stream, however, is daunting hazard for those who have hit a subpar tee ball.

If the hole is played correctly, two good efforts leave a short shot into the green that is cantered back to front and perched high enough that only a portion of the flagstick is visible.

The round over, there is no clubhouse to retire to, but the stone parking lot is an ideal spot to recount the triumphs and tribulations.

BEYOND THE GREEN

The Davis Museum at Wellesley College is one of the oldest fine art museums in the United States, founded more than 120 years ago by the first President of Wellesley College.

According to the website, "The Davis collections, which span global history from antiquity to the present and include masterpieces from almost every continent, are housed today in an extraordinary museum building, designed by Rafael Moneo, winner of the Pritzker Architecture Prize."

CHAPTER 22

Northwood Golf Club, Monte Rio, Calif.

There is no doubt that Alister Mackenzie is one of the finest golf course architects ever to lay out a course. The point could be made that he is *the* finest. Although most of his creations are private and exclusive, there is a smattering of Mackenzie creations that the average golfer can experience.

One of those is Mackenzie's only nine-hole design in North America, Northwood Golf Club in Monte Rio, California, about 80 miles north San Francisco in the Russian River Valley.

Adding to the joy and the uniqueness of the layout is the fact it is carved out of a redwood forest. What will mostly likely stun first-time visitors is not just the size of the behemoths, but the fact that they are not old-growth trees but have risen to the immense proportions since 1928 when the course opened.

For the golfer looking to escape the world, Northwood is an ideal location, a self-contained respite from the racing rats.

Arrive at the pro shop, park the car, and within a walk of no more than sixty seconds is a restaurant, coffee shop, post office, barber, and a motel with a pool. Cell service can be iffy, at best.

As for the golf course, the layout retains much of the original design. Unfortunately, hole corridors have narrowed over the years as the Redwoods expanded. Their protected status and the cost of logging make removal difficult. Northwood remains, however, a delight to play at 2,888 yards and a par of 36.

Although narrow at times, Northwood is never without strategy or challenges. The assortment of holes, including three par-4s under 295 yards, test all aspects of a player's game, from accuracy with longer clubs to adroitness with the shorter ones.

The first hole is abridged slightly from the original, as the tee was brought forward when the restaurant was built more than thirty years ago.

Two of Northwood's permanent residents reside behind the seventh green. From a distance, when they are adorned with golf hats, the carvings are often mistaken for people. (*Anthony Pioppi*)

The length is 290 yards with a fairway that bends to the left and tee shots carrying the remnants of an original centerline bunker that would be wonderful if restored.

Laying up is the prudent play, as two bunkers in the right watch over the narrowing fairway at about 220 yards.

The green is a Mackenzie gem. The front tilts toward the line of play, the back away, and the entire left side falls off hard while the back right corner rises slightly.

Golfers get their first taste of Redwoods on the second hole, which has a par of four and is 383 yards. The enormous trees run down the right side. The fairway opens somewhat to the left, but that side has its perils as well with out-of-bounds off the tee.

From about 135 yards from the middle of the green, the flattish fairway morphs into one with rolls and humps, ending at an intricate green. Miss the putting surface left, and the golf ball can find its way to the third hole, while the right side is more forgiving as is it is bowled up and guides shots to the putting surface. The back left corner rises while the back right drops off sharply.

The par-3 third has the only completely nonoriginal putting surface at Northwood, Mackenzie's having been washed away by the flooded waters of the Russian River a number of years ago. The green is the least appealing on the layout. The hole is 145 yards with out-of-bounds beyond the green.

Mackenzie produced a challenging drivable par-4 at 292 yards for the fourth hole, a slight dogleg right. The entire left side of the hole corridor is out-of-bounds, as the yards of the homes on Redwood Drive are flush to the fairway, replacing what was originally a line of redwoods.

Not a bunker guards the long narrow green, but it is elevated, and shots that fail to find the target can bound a good distance away.

At 464 yards, the fifth hole is the first par-5 five of the day, and while it may be considered short, only the straightest of hitters will be going for the green in two, as the ever-present Redwoods border the hole on both sides almost the entire way. On the left, there are also homes and white out-of-bounds stakes.

The sagacious play is to leave the woods in the bag and go with a long iron off the tee and a midiron on the second shot in order to minimize the chances of encountering significant trouble.

On the left side of the green two bunkers are carved out of the fill pad, while the right side is only rough.

Two spines parallel to the line of play make this a fun green to putt.

Mackenzie's last short four is a dandy, with the tee set back near the first green. The hole curls to the right. For the golfer who has thoughts of playing down the first fairway, a tree expertly placed near the green makes that a poor choice.

Looking across the sixth green and down the seventh fairway shows off two of the defining characteristics of Northwood, the intricate Mackenzie green complexes and the redwoods. (*Anthony Pioppi*)

On the right side of the sixth, which borders the starting hole, a series of mounds penalizes the overcooked shot. Another mound about 65 yards from the green and a Mackenzie depression create awkward stances for those unlucky to find their golf ball there. At the same time the fairway falls toward the putting surface, so shots can be run on to the green.

The green complex is longer than it is wide and unforgiving to the missed approach, as it drops off hard to the left, right, and rear. An interior bowl on the putting surface collects successful approaches.

Seven is the bear hole, as two of the creatures carved out of large stumps stand guard behind the green of the 381-yard hole. Occasionally, they have been known to don golf hats.

The hole corridor is narrow and bunkers short left and right protect the green, which mostly runs back to front. The far edge of the putting surface tilts away from the line of play and will send overly aggressive shots far into the rough.

Some years back, the eighth hole was shortened to get the tee out of the line of fire of the ninth, a wise move. It now measures 120 yards, but the hole plays shorter as a result of the elevation decline from the tee to the putting surface. Four bunkers, the most on any hole, guard the kidney-shaped green.

To the left of the ninth tee, through the trees and on the other side of the winding Russian River, is the Bohemian Grove, a summer retreat for members of the Bohemian Club in San Francisco. Founded by journalists, artists, and musicians in 1872, the all-male membership is now made up of some of the most powerful business and political people in the country.

Bohemian Club member Jack Neville was the impetus for the founding of Northwood. Neville won the California Amateur Championship five times. An accomplished golf course architect, Neville codesigned Pebble Beach Golf Links.

Northwood's closing hole is akin to the previous par-5. A narrow affair, so putting away the long clubs in favor of the conservative play is the prudent decision on the 533-yard hole.

The fairway ascends a slope, creating the only blind tee shot of the round with homes on the left and the ubiquitous redwoods on the right.

Leading into the putting surface, the fairway drops and then rises up to a green that is in the original location but is not wholly a Mackenzie design, having been softened somewhat years ago.

Still, it fits in with the overall scheme and is an appropriate way to end the round on such a distinctive layout.

BEYOND THE GREEN

The small town of Guerneville is a quick drive from Northwood. A gay-friendly locale dating back to the 1970s, the town, for its size, has a ridiculous number of restaurants worth visiting, from fine dining to great hamburgers.

Seek out the Stumptown Brewery. Stumptown makes its own beer, but this is a local bar and not an upscale tasting experience. Go for the Rat Bastard Pale Ale and the Blimey the Wanker E.S.B. Skip the free pizza.

Korbel Champagne cellars are not far away. Within another thirty minutes or so are fifty more wineries.

Head west, and shortly you come to the Sonoma Coast, including where the Russian River meets the Pacific Ocean.

CHAPTER 23

Winter Park Golf Course, Winter Park, Fla.

The Winter Park Golf Course is one of those funky layouts that harks back to a time when golf courses were part of the community, literally. The layout is broken into five parcels and requires six crossings of tree-lined streets and avenues that border nearly every hole. Out-of-bounds stakes delineate the fairways from the yards of adjacent homes.

While negotiating Winter Park, golfers go through and along neighborhoods and up to an active rail line. The Winter Park walk even takes golfers past two churches and a cemetery.

The layout is 2,480 yards and has a par of 34 with three par-3s, five par-4s, and one par-5. Three of the par-4s are drivable. Winter Park is the shortest of the finest nine-hole golf courses in North America. It is also the only facility on the list that has eighteen holes—but more on that later.

In terms of distance, the layout has changed little in the ninety-plus years of existence. The 1916 edition of *The American Annual Golf Guide* listed Winter Park as 2,261 yards. In terms of design, though, what was and what is are worlds apart.

The original nine-hole private course opened in 1914 and was part of the overall land plan devised by Winter Park's founders. A year later, eighteen holes were added; they wrapped around the existing nine. The entire facility closed in 1926. Another club had opened in town and, as a result, rounds at Winter Park fell off severely.

When that club went under, Winter Park was reorganized on its original site in 1937, once again as a nine-hole facility, and has remained in continuous operation since then.

Before 2016, Winter Park was a flat golf course, including the small roundish greens, and had few bunkers.

When the city decided to make significant improvements, it hired the design duo of Riley Johns and Keith Rhebb, who each run their own golf course architectural

Winter Park's Golf Pro Shop Manager Gregg Pascale watches his bunker shot on the sixth hole as a SunRail commuter train rolls by a short distance away. Trains regularly pass the golf course. (*Anthony Pioppi*)

firms but came together for the Winter Park project. Johns called it a "creative collaboration, artistic partnership" and a "joint venture."

However you want to term the team, it was an unqualified success.

The duo moved earth on nearly every square millimeter of the site, rebuilding tees, constructing all new greens that are larger and much more entertaining than their predecessors, and adding bumps, mounds, and humps to the fairways.

In a stroke of genius, it was decided there would be no rough at Winter Park. One height of cut encompasses fairways, tees, and approaches. (Whoever was responsible for the suggestion and/or decision, please stand up and take a well-deserved bow.)

Rhebb and Johns also added a number of elements to increase the strategy required in playing every hole.

Take the first, a par-4 of 240 yards with East Webster Avenue running down the entire right side. The hole is drivable, but to dissuade golfers from taking a path next to the road, a greenside bunker was placed on that side. The left side, on the other hand, is wide open, so even for those not going for it in one, the strategy is to play away from Webster.

The elevated green with its ridges and slopes heralds what is to come—challenging and fun putting surfaces.

The second is 146 yards, and to get to the tee requires a walk across North Park Avenue. Two bunkers guard the green with a small opening between the pair, but missing left allows for an open approach on the ground or through the air. The putting surface has a small hump in the middle that has an effect on most putts. A rise holds up the back and serves to stop shots that might go long.

A turn to the right, and a few steps across North Webster Avenue takes golfers to the third hole, a 430-yard island amidst a sea of thoroughfares, the aforementioned North Webster along with Keys, West Stovin, and North New York. The fourth is the only hole on this parcel.

The strategy is simple to understand, but not easy to utilize. Challenge the fairway bunker on the left, and the green opens up from that side. Take the wider route to the right, and risk being blocked by a notch of trees and/or having to negotiate a bunker on the shot to the green.

The par-3 eighth hole has a green that golfers can approach via the air or ground. A miss left or right leaves the player with a difficult up-and-down for par. (*Anthony Pioppi*)

The putting surface falls from front left to back right but has all sorts of other features throughout.

The jaunt to the fourth requires walking across North New York and back some 200 yards, as well as passing First Winter Park Baptist Church.

A few more steps and there is the fourth hole; bordering the left side is Palm Cemetery.

"Hit it in there and you know what you are?" Winter Park golf pro shop manager Gregg Pascale asks. Before his partner can respond he answers, "dead," and laughs a little too hard at his own joke.

He then proceeds to launch his next two drives onto the graves.

The 495-yard dogleg left bends around the final resting place for hundreds of souls. On the side of the turn, a large bunker guards the preferential route. For the tee balls that end left and short of the bunker, the logical play is to dance with death and play over the graves, mausoleums, and a hedgerow. Rhebb and Johns upped the ante, adding a demoniacal surprise on the other side of the shrub line and out of view, a bunker that serves to snare what appeared to be the perfect shot that has seemingly flown past all the trouble.

Here, the longer hitters can get home in two, but the elevated putting surface with a bunker left and right and sharp back edge that sends overplayed efforts tumbling away makes the goal a difficult one to obtain, but it is one that can be achieved.

After crossing West Webster Avenue, the fifth at 354 yards awaits, with cemetery and road to the left as well as trees left and right. Two bunkers to the left dominate the player's eye.

The putting surface is of the potato chip variety with the flattish right and left portions higher than the middle, creating a sort of mini punchbowl. It is the only green without bunkers.

Go too long, and the shot could come to a stop on North New York Ave.

The sixth hole introduces the golfers to another part of the fun of playing Winter Park, an active rail line over which Amtrak and SunRail trains roll.

Even without the added entertainment the hole is a fun one, full of choices. It's 262 yards with a grove of trees to the right, and more trees and out-of-bounds area to the left. The tracks run close enough to the green that a tee ball too far to that side can find the steel rails, wooden ties, and jagged stones.

The green is drivable, however, with a bold shot over the trees or by bending the shot around. Sand guards the putting surface front left, and a marvelous Lion's Mouth-style bunker protects the right front. There is plenty of space to miss the green to that side, and a steep back ridge is there to rein in overly bold shots.

The seventh hole is Winter Park's longest par-3 at 179 yards with the tees close enough to the passing trains that you get the feeling a conductor could reach out the window and punch your ticket as he passed.

Three bunkers guard the green left, while the right side is open with a Redan-like kick slope to direct shots onto the putting surface, but the slope can also send shots over the green and close to the nearby road.

The eighth hole is similar to the second, 145 yards compared to 146.

Three left side bunkers guard the green. On the right, the side rises up enough so that it can be used by savvy golfers to guide a low-running golf ball onto the carpet.

As with the opening hole, the final act of Winter Park is a drivable four. It comes in at 245 yards and seems easy to reach, but an abundance of afflictions await the poor shot.

The hole bends slightly left and trees guard that side. Five bunkers, the most on any hole at Winter Park, have their say. The largest is 45 yards short of the middle of the green. Staggered down the right is a necklace of three white sand pearls. Overshooting them means finding the driveway leading to the Casa Feliz Historic Home and Museum, or worse. The restored Spanish Farmhouse designed by James Gamble Rogers II is a popular wedding venue. Want to see some angry people? Drop your tee ball into the middle of the nuptial ceremony.

Behind the green is a small bunker not visible from the fairway; beyond that is the course's parking lot.

The walk along the ninth brings golfers past the second house of worship, the First Church of Christ Scientist, Winter Park.

"Golfers have two chances to pray to the golf gods for help," Pascale says smiling. He doesn't mention anything about asking for forgiveness.

The other nine holes at Winter Park—known as The Back 9 Putting Course—are found adjacent to the ninth tee. The large putting/chipping green has nine flags and nine rules, including no. 2, "no gimmes." Anyone is free to walk on and have a go as long as they are courteous to other players (rule no. 9).

Things to Do

So if Disney and Orlando is not your idea of fun, Winter Park has plenty to offer.

There is an hour-long Winter Park Scenic Boat Tour that takes passengers on three of the seven lakes that make up the Winter Park chain. There are views of whooping cranes, alligators, subtropical flowers, and multimillion-dollar estates and homes.

Each April, the Albin Polasek Museum & Sculpture Gardens hosts its weeklong Winter Park Paint Out. Twenty-five professionally acclaimed plein air artists roam across the city "capturing many of your favorite landscapes and landmarks with oils, watercolors and pastels."

Plein Air—a French term meaning "in the open air"—describes artwork painted outdoors with the subject in front of the artist.

The Polasek Museum "holds an art collection focusing primarily on American representational sculpture, with over 200 works by Czech-born American sculptor Albin Polasek."

The museum consists of the Polasek residence and chapel, an outdoor sculpture garden, and a gallery with rotating exhibits.

The museum is listed on the National Register of Historic Places and is one of the thirty-four members of the National Trust's Historic Artists' Homes and Studios.

Chapter 24

Uplands Golf and Ski Club, Thornhill, ON, Canada

For much of its existence, what is now known as Uplands Golf and Ski Club was an eighteen-hole private layout, not a snobbish country club, but a place where good golfers roamed and a place that featured one of the greatest par-3 holes in the Western Hemisphere.

Canadian golf writer Lorne Rubenstein, a former member of what was then called Uplands Golf and Country Club, wrote lovingly about the original layout that barely snuck past 6,000 yards in Mike Bell's book *The Golf Courses of Stanley Thompson: Celebrating Canada's Historic Masterpieces*:

"The funky old Stanley Thompson course offered uneven lies from start to finish, greens perched on headlands across valleys, greens in bowls, and, always, a stern test of shot making."

Ted Tom, the golf course superintendent in his second stint at the club, said that when Uplands was private and eighteen holes it was a club for the blue-collar crowd, "but all good players, so many sidehill and uphill lies."

Uplands has a significant design pedigree. Legendary Canadian golf course designer Thompson, a founding member of the America Society of Golf Course Architects, laid out Uplands, which opened in the mid-1920s.

"It was the poor man's Stanley Thompson private club," Tom said.

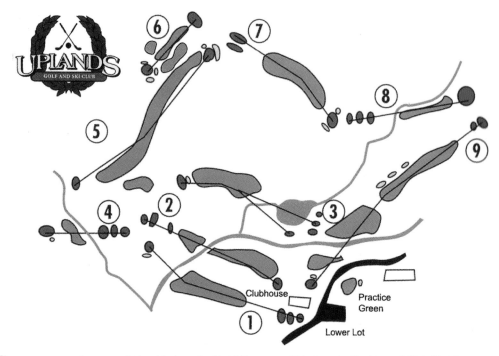

The scorecard map of the Uplands Golf Course. (*Uplands Golf and Ski Club*)

In 1989, the owner of Uplands converted half the property to home lots, including a large chunk he saved for himself and on which he constructed his massive house that overlooks the remaining nine holes.

According to Tom, who is also a college professor, the original plan was to convert the undeveloped part of the course to a park. When the owner decided to keep the golf holes, the municipality purchased the land and made it a public facility. A management company that also oversees the ski hill in the center of the property runs it.

This is Tom's second stint as the Uplands superintendent. He was there from 1975 until the club was sold off in 1989, returning in 2010.

When the course was split, no thought went into how to best keep a contiguous nine, since retaining golf was not in the plans. Today what exists is a combination of holes—some from the original front nine, some from the original back nine, as well as some that are a combination of former holes.

There are some interesting characteristics about Uplands, one being that it borders Thornhill Golf Club, which in turn is separated by a four-lane road from Ladies Golf Club of Toronto, all Thompson designs that opened between 1922 and 1926.

A trait of Uplands that seems to go against Thompson's style is the dearth of bunkers; there are fewer than a dozen. According to Tom, in a weird quirk, many more sand hazards were found on the portion of the design that was sacrificed for real estate.

The first hole is a par-4 of 360 yards, but a stream running across the fairway at about 240 yards forces most players to lay up. The elevation change from fairway to green calls for a club or more to be added on the approach shot.

The green comes nearly up against the third hole of the Thornhill Club, which is on the other side of a stone wall, a thin line of trees, and undergrowth.

Uplands' second hole, originally the ninth, plays opposite of the first. It tees off from the top of the hill and drops significantly as it plays back toward the clubhouse. The hole is 325 yards. For golfers with abundant length, the green can be driven.

According to Tom, the story is that during the Second World War the course was closed and used for tank driving training because of the severe and substantial elevation changes such as those found on the second hole.

The third hole runs in the same direction as the first but does not climb all the way up the ridge, although the green is higher than the tee. It is 332 yards and can be driven, as well, but in order to do that the line of play must be directly at the green, and that is a route rife with danger, namely, trees that line the corridor.

Because the original green was so small, approximately 2,000 square feet, Tom converted an area near the putting surface into green, creating a shelf.

For reasons unknown, Tom said the third fairway is unlike any other on the property. Not only does it heave more in the Canadian winter than the others, but also it holds water so well during the playing season that it never needs irrigation, subsisting on what nature delivers in the way of rain.

The first par-3 of the day, the fourth hole, was originally the second hole. It plays only 113 yards but is a tester with a bunker left.

A stream in front of the ninth green is the chief concern for those golfers attempting to reach the par-5 ninth green in two blows. (*Bryan Moran*)

Immediately on the other side of the trees behind the putting surface is another Thornhill green.

A combination of two holes was used to make up the fifth hole, a par-4 of 350 yards. The fairway and green were part of the former eleventh, but the tee is from the former third hole.

Running across the top of a ridge, the fairway rolls more than any other on the course, ending at a green protected in back and to the left by bunkers.

The sixth hole is another par-3 and the only uncomfortable spot in the makeshift routing. It plays 150 yards in the opposite direction of the previous hole, and the putting surface has three bunkers around it. The two on the left are originals. The green was originally from the fifth hole and was played in a different direction from the current setup.

The problem comes after the hole is finished. Golfers must walk back the entire length of the sixth in order to get to the tee of the par-4 310-yard seventh. On that hole, the fairway and the green are from the original routing; it had been the sixteenth hole, but the tee was relocated up and well left of the original location, making the dogleg right much less severe and the hole shorter.

A bunker short right and another left guard the green.

Then there is the eighth, the hole for which Uplands has garnered attention and acclaim.

The 232-yarder, originally the seventeenth, starts from an elevated tee across a deep valley to an elevated green benched into the side of a hill. Trees guard the right and wrap around the back. The face of the green complex is severe. Shots that land short and left will run well away from the target. The play, according to Tom, is to fly the tee shot into the turf wall right of the green and let the ball tumble onto the putting surface, which for a hole of that length is undersized.

It appears, though, that the eighth in its present form is not the original. Tom said club lore has it that Stanley Thompson's brother made adjustments to the layout early in its life and extending the tee back at this hole was one of those changes. Lending credence to the story is the fact that Tom discovered an above-ground irrigation line that runs up to an overgrown level area—most certainly a teeing site—well forward and left of the existing tee. The hole would have played at approximately 170 yards.

Uplands concludes with a reachable par-5, originally the eighteenth hole, and requires the crossing of a stream and the road leading to the skiing area.

Tom said most players lay up and then make the decision of whether to go for the green or play it safe. There is one bunker, and it is short and right of the putting surface, which canters severely from back to front, with more tilt than any other green on the layout.

BEYOND THE GREEN

Located 10 about miles north of downtown Toronto, Thornhill is officially designated a Greater Toronto Area neighborhood.

   The chief attraction is the Promenade shopping mall, with over 150 stores. There is also the Heintzman House, which was completed in 1802 and is one of the oldest buildings in the area. Throughout the course of the year the Heintzman hosts such events as an art show and sale, a craft show, and Christmas caroling.

   If playing another finest nine is the desire, Allandale Golf Course (see Chapter 17) in Innisfil, Ontario, is approximately a fifty-mile drive away.

CHAPTER 25

Hotchkiss School Golf Course, Salisbury, Conn.

The Course at Yale is arguably Seth Raynor's finest design, opening in April 1926, three months after his unexpected death.

Unknown to many is the fact that while Yale was being built another Raynor course in Connecticut was under construction, this one a nine-hole layout in the far northwest corner of the state, and it too was created for an institution of learning.

Some sixty-five miles from New Haven and the Yale campus is the exclusive Hotchkiss School, a private preparatory boarding school, and it is here that Raynor's finest surviving nine is located. It is also here that Raynor met Charles "Josh" Banks, the head of Hotchkiss fundraising who had graduated from Hotchkiss (1902) and then Yale (1906).

After meeting Raynor as part of the Hotchkiss project, Banks departed the only place he had ever worked as an adult to join Raynor's firm in 1925 even though he had no experience in the field prior to the Hotchkiss project. In short order, Banks was listed as a partner, the only one Raynor ever had.

When Raynor passed away, it was Banks who finished many of Raynor's jobs in progress including the course at the Fishers Island Club, before going on to his own notable but brief design career, including work at Hotchkiss.

In the 1930s, when the town of Salisbury widened a road forcing a redesign on a portion of the Hotchkiss course, it was Banks who returned to his alma mater to reconfigure the layout. He passed away before the project was complete.

Except for two greens, the existing Hotchkiss course is a Raynor-Banks hybrid.

It is unknown how many nine-hole layouts Raynor designed or were built, and no others besides Hotchkiss are known to exist.

Raynor's finest nine was Ocean Links, constructed with his mentor Charles Blair Macdonald serving the role as consultant. The layout bordered Newport (R.I.) Country Club. It had a brief life, opening in 1919 and closing for good in 1941.

Down the road from Hotchkiss another private prep institution, the Taft School, also had a Raynor nine-hole design commissioned at the same time as Hotchkiss, but for reasons unknown the school delayed constructing the course. It was built without Raynor's input and apparently not exactly to the plans. In its short existence, the Taft course was altered many times and subsequently abandoned. Two greens of the original layout remain, though, and are found on the practice area of the Watertown Golf Club.

What Raynor originally created at Hotchkiss stood with his best work. Aerial photography from the early- and mid-1930s shows large, bold green complexes defended by yawning bunkers and strategy throughout. This was no second-rate effort.

Unfortunately, though, for years Hotchkiss has put the barest of effort into maintaining and preserving Raynor's achievement. There is no dedicated golf course superintendent; the staff that maintains the turf throughout the rest of the Hotchkiss campus also cares for the layout. As a result, putting surfaces have shrunk dramatically; some are perhaps a third of their original dimensions. Bunkers, too, have dwindled in size or been filled in. Because of construction and expansion of school buildings, holes have been shortened.

Hotchkiss would benefit more than any other layout in the top 25 mentioned in this book from a significant restoration and an increase in the quality of daily course maintenance. It is another Culver Academy (ranked No. 3) waiting to happen. Enough of the bones and meat of the Raynor-Banks design are there, though, to warrant Hotckiss's inclusion on the list of finest nines.

The course, 3,040 yards with a par of 35, begins with a brute of a hole, which was not Raynor's intent; it was the third hole of the original routing.

On the Raynor design, the green sat to the left of where it does now. When the state relocated the nearby road to the current location, moving the putting surface was necessitated. The new green was opened in 1931. Banks died earlier that year of a heart attack shortly after returning from a work trip to Bermuda.

The current incarnation of the first hole is most likely based on what Raynor designed originally, since the landform it sits on is the same. The uphill two-shot Reverse Redan, with the fairway leaning hard left to right, plays much longer than its 420 yards.

With uneven lies in the fairway, a road running the length of the hole, a bunker short left of the green, and a dramatic fall-off on the right side of the putting surface, starting the round with a large number is easy to do.

The second tee is a 300-yard walk from the first green, but it is an enjoyable stroll that takes golfers across Interlaken Road, through the main entrance of the school and Scoville Gate, and then past the three massive statues of relaxing bovines, Peter Woytuk's work called *Three Bulls.*

When the course opened, the second hole played as a par-4 of 256 yards. Years later, a new set of tees was added that allowed it to also be played as a par-3 of 195 yards. After the construction of a gymnasium over the course of the last twenty years, the second hole was permanently reduced to a par-3 of 173 yards.

As a par-4, this was a Leven Hole, one of the many templates Raynor used in his designs. Mounding in front of the right corner of the green requires the use of strategy, as it blocks the golfers' view of the putting surface. To see the green on the approach, then, the tee balls must be played down the left side and flirt with disaster in the form of Sharon Road, which runs along the length of the entire second hole.

On the putting surface, a pronounced spine runs from right front corner toward the back left, tapering off in the middle. Another significant ridge extends from the back left toward the middle of the putting surface before dissipating. The two never meet.

At 390 yards, the third hole is another template, an Alps-Punchbowl Hole. Originally two bunkers were dug out in front of the green, forcing players to fly their

The second hole at the Hotchkiss School Golf Course features a green that stands with some of architect Seth Raynor's best. Two prominent spines give the putting surface its character and charm. (*Peter Barrett*)

approach onto the putting surface, but now only the one on the left remains, which means the play is down the right side and away from Sharon Road.

The Punchbowl feature is reminiscent of the one at Fox Chapel Golf Club in Pittsburg. Two diabolical ridges run through the green almost horizontal to the line of play, adding excitement to putting.

Crossing the road and the fourth hole, golfers find an uphill par-4 of 370 yards, which includes one of the two greens at Hotchkiss not built by Raynor or Banks.

When Raynor designed the Hotchkiss course, he used one green complex from the Robert Pryde-designed layout. It tilted severely—almost too severely—back to front, and its style didn't meld with the other eight. Why Raynor chose to retain the green is unknown. Perhaps it was a favorite of the headmaster, who overruled Raynor's plan.

In the early 2000s, the green was relocated to accommodate dorm construction. Raynor historian George Bahto designed a new putting surface, which fits with the land and the hole.

The entire fourth hole tilts left to right with thick woods on the right. On the left a fairway bunker awaits, and behind that is student housing.

A deep bunker right and short guards the green that has a mild hog's back feature in it.

Arguably the best view on the Hotchkiss course is from the fifth tee with Lake Wononscopomuc below and the hills of Northwest Connecticut beyond the shimmering blue water.

Five is also a template, called Short; it is par-3 that at Hotchkiss measures 140 yards. For their short holes, Raynor and Banks almost always nearly surrounded a large, elevated green complex with sand, so missing the target resulted in a difficult recovery. A mildly off-line tee shot that stops on the carpet means a long treacherous putt that many times must go through the "thumb print" impression found on most Short Hole greens.

For the Hotchkiss version, Raynor modified the concept for the site. Originally, a large bunker, a portion of which remains, wrapped around much of the front of the putting surface. Guarding the remaining portion of the green, in place of the usual sand, are severe slopes that send errant shots careening away.

Playing at 358 yards, the uphill sixth bends to the left, coming to its conclusion at a fantastic green, the defining characteristic of the hole.

A strip bunker right and a smaller bunker short left protect the putting surface that is divided into three portions by a t-shaped ridge and what may be the only example on a Raynor green where the back portion is below the front.

An aerial view from the early 1930s shows the current second and third holes of the Hotchkiss School Golf Course as they were originally constructed. (*Hotchkiss Archives & Special Collection*)

At one point, this may have been a Road Hole green, based on the seventeenth hole at the Old Course in St. Andrews, Scotland, but with the original bunkering gone it is difficult to tell.

This is a Time Out Green, which is such a delight that once the hole is over golfers will invariably find themselves challenging the tantalizing features with a few extra rolls.

At one time the seventh played as a par-5 of 500 yards or a par-4 of 440, but the addition of a school building removed the dual role, making it permanently a 465-yard three-shotter.

The green is not an original and is the least interesting at Hotchkiss. The rerouting of the school's main entrance decades ago facilitated the relocation of the putting surface, which occurred after Raynor and Banks were dead.

Out-of-bounds in the guise of Interlaken Road parallel the entire right side of the hole. The fairway has a left-to-right canter, so taking it up the left is preferred, but trees planted to protect buildings make that a difficult task. The conservative choice of playing a hybrid or even a midiron off the tree is the pragmatic way to deal with the seventh, since it leaves little room for error.

The original first hole, the par-3 eighth, is a double Raynor rarity.

Hotchkiss's Eden Hole is 189 yards, and the green resides at least one club in distance below the tee. The design is patterned after the eleventh hole at the Old Course in St. Andrews.

It is one of the few Raynor Edens that plays downhill. The large putting surface has a protrusion, another rarity, that is big enough and flat enough to accommodate hole locations.

A bunker that runs across the front of the putting surface is not entirely original. It was at least a third smaller when the hole opened.

Hotchkiss's ninth hole bears little resemblance to the one that Raynor designed. Originally, it paralleled the first, but when that hole was shifted to make way for the road, Banks moved the ninth tee and fairway but left the green. He also bunkered the putting surface differently, converting what may have been a Cape Hole Green into a Road Hole-style.

Where the ninth most likely was a dogleg left with a downhill shot into the green to begin with, the current form of the 533-yard hole is a sharp bend to the right off the tee and then significantly uphill for the next two blows. The green, which has the road bunker to the right, falls off so sharply to the left that golf balls can be sent caroming into thick overgrowth. The practice green and the tiny, quaint pro shop can be found past the putting surface.

The view from behind the ninth green at the Hotchkiss School Golf Course—with the existing fairway on the right, and the former fairway on the left, now part of the first hole, that was used before a road expansion altered the layout. (*Peter Barrett*)

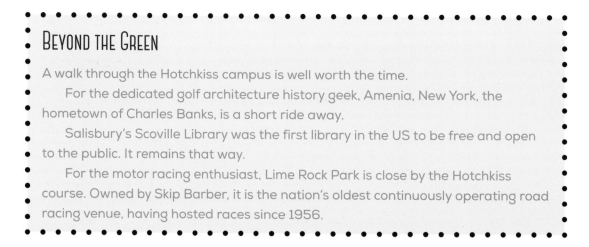

Beyond the Green

A walk through the Hotchkiss campus is well worth the time.

For the dedicated golf architecture history geek, Amenia, New York, the hometown of Charles Banks, is a short ride away.

Salisbury's Scoville Library was the first library in the US to be free and open to the public. It remains that way.

For the motor racing enthusiast, Lime Rock Park is close by the Hotchkiss course. Owned by Skip Barber, it is the nation's oldest continuously operating road racing venue, having hosted races since 1956.

CHAPTER 26

Designing a Nine-Hole Golf Course in the Modern Age

Golf course architect Mike Nuzzo finds himself in a rare spot. He has been called upon to design a nine-hole golf course, not a par-3 or executive layout, but one with par-4s and par-5s as well that will never expand to eighteen holes. His plans call for the course to play from 1,500 yards to 3,200 yards, with the goal to bring enjoyment to every class of player. It is hoped that the course will open in the spring of 2018.

Nuzzo's creation will offer innumerable challenges from round to round, never mind day-to-day, as he incorporated the ditches and streams that run through the property into the routing, producing strategic, challenging golf holes.

Called Nine Grand Golf Course, it is part of the Grand Oaks Reserve, which will, if all goes to plan, rise from the Texas plains in the tiny town of Cleveland, 45 miles northwest of Houston. There will be 1,000 homes, 250 condominiums, 400 apartments, and a nine-hole golf course.

According to Nuzzo, before he set about creating the layout, the owner established one guideline: make the course "fun" for everyone.

Nuzzo was given that charge once before and built his best-known design, the eighteen-hole ultraprivate Wolf Point Ranch Club in Port Lacava, Texas, about 130 miles southeast of Houston on the Gulf of Mexico. It has wide fairways and large greens with multiple routes to play each hole, but only one or two that will yield the best score to the bold and accurate golfer. Nine Grand incorporates precisely the same concept.

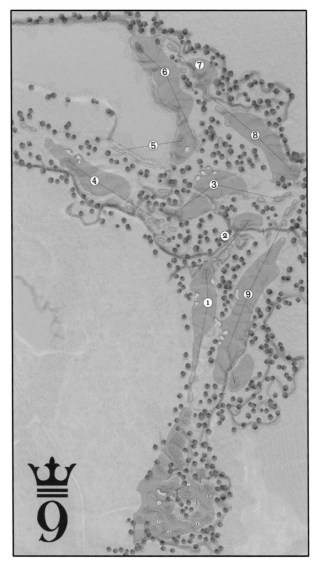

Mike Nuzzo's plans for Nine Grand Golf Course includes a routing that also lets golfers play loops of three and seven holes. In addition, there is a nine-hole par-3 course and a large putting green. (*Mike Nuzzo*)

When building an affordable golf course, enjoyment has to be the top priority. For Nine Grand that means entertaining people, including nongolfers. There will be a nine-hole par-3 course along with a large putting course that abounds in undulations.

Residents of the development will be able to use the practice areas whether they are golfers or not, and the clubhouse will double as a community center. The aim is not to merely attract people to the game, but to also create family-friendly activities and a positive environment around the game of golf.

In a novel approach, Nine Grand will have options for golfers based on time. According to Nuzzo, if a player has thirty minutes, then the putting course will be suggested. If there are sixty minutes to spare, then the par-3 layout is perfect. For those who have two hours on their hands, then playing all the holes on Nine Grand is the way to go. Complete all three courses in succession, and it will be known as a Grand Slam.

Those who do play the big course will encounter a layout that is welcoming to all skill levels. Tees will stretch great lengths so that shorter hitters will feel comfortable and longer hitters will be tested. Fairways will have up to 90 yards of width, but there will be optimal angles into greens for those chasing a score. Because the putting surfaces are large, averaging 8,000 square feet more than double the most common greens, the location of the flagstick will alter the strategy for approach shots.

According to Nuzzo, the natural contours of the site are ideal for a golf course.

"In truth, there is no earthwork—only minor shaping," he wrote in an email.

In a neat twist, rounds do not have to be nine or eighteen holes. From the first tee, players can take advantage of a three-hole or seven-hole loop, or for that matter, a twelve-hole or sixteen-hole round. Golfers can walk from the second green to the third or ninth tees and later in the round walk from the fifth tee to the ninth tee, skipping holes six and seven.

Nuzzo sees a measurable difference when it comes to designing a nine-hole layout compared to one with eighteen holes. Nine offers him the chance to be more creative, especially at Nine Grand, where there is far more acreage than needed for the course.

"With nine holes because you can do anything, it allows me to be more efficient with the land," Nuzzo said.

Because he had choices and his hand was free, Nuzzo created a routing he said flows naturally to the point that it should be inviting even to nongolfers.

"I want someone to *want* to walk this," he said.

Nuzzo incorporated boundless variety into his creation. Along with the massive fairways and greens, there is a multitude of teeing grounds on each hole. For instance, the par-3 fifth plays from 130 yards to 230 yards and 75 yards from an informal teeing ground, which has no forced carry over water like the others on the hole.

"You have angles and yardages to play with," Nuzzo said. "Each hole you'd like to play quite different every day."

It is a sound concept, a design where the stated goal is creating the utmost pleasure for the widest variety of golfers.

If Nuzzo's vision comes to fruition, it surely will be one of the finest nines, and a model for others to follow.

CHAPTER **27**

Odd Ones In

Golf courses that don't fit the traditional model, with neither nine nor eighteen holes (nor even an increment of nine), are scattered throughout North America.

They are, though, standard layouts in every other sense of the word, with holes that have pars of three, four, and five, and provide a place for golfers to tee it up and enjoy themselves.

Some of the layouts have interesting tales regarding how they came to have an unorthodox existence, while for others the reason for the uniqueness is long forgotten.

One example is the six-hole **Silver Spring Golf Course** in East Providence, R.I. Much of the history of Silver Spring is known, thanks to the research of course superintendent Dick Silva.

When it began in 1898, the layout was called the Silver Spring Country Club. There were six holes, the club was private, the membership was made up of prominent citizens, and there were caddies to carry your clubs.

Then in 1917 Standard Oil purchased the land but let the golf club continue. Silver Spring would pay no rent, but, according to a *Providence Magazine* article from 1922, "the office force of Standard Oil Company, and such other employees as might be designated, were to be members of the club."

Frank E. McBride, who went on to win the Rhode Island state golf championship while a member, was one of the Standard people who played out of Silver Spring.

Providence is a deepwater port. Standard purchased the land to give its tankers a place to unload. As a result, a massive pipeline that was installed by Standard, and that still runs through the layout, was incorporated into the design. According to a magazine, dirt was heaped "so covering the pipes that a big bunker would extend from east to west."

Standard, according to the publication, also put substantial money into improving Silver Spring, and it appears that at that time the layout was expanded to nine holes.

Years later, the area where the three new holes were located was deemed to be the ideal location for large storage tanks, and Silver Spring reverted to six holes. The tanks were subsequently removed, but no effort has been made by ExxonMobil—the company Standard became—to create three more holes.

A few years ago, Silver Spring grounds crew members uncovered an old green, which was revived. The layout now has six holes but seven greens.

The large series of pipes remains, running from the dock, through the course, and on to a large storage facility nearly a mile away. At least three times a week the tankers' cargo of diesel, ethanol, or gasoline flows under the course.

Silver Springs is easily played as more than a six-hole course. Silva has set it up so that there are two flags on the greens for the second to eighth and third to ninth holes. Also, with fifteen teeing grounds, many holes have a variety of yardages and angles.

The nine-hole routing plays 2,400 yards from the white tees and 1,900 yards from the yellows.

Silva also uncovered the fact that it was Silver Spring members who traveled roughly five miles north and founded the famed Wannamoisett Country Club. The Donald Ross golf course opened in 1914.

In Jefferson, Wisconsin, there is a thirteen-hole layout that began its existence as nine holes.

According to head golf professional/general manager Brad Calaway, what is now the public **Jefferson Golf Course** was the private Meadow Springs Country Club.

Jefferson is halfway between the state's two biggest cities, Milwaukee and Madison. In the early 1920s, judges from those municipalities would come to Jefferson once a week to hear cases, and it was the black-robed men who essentially demanded a golf course.

In 1997 the club was purchased and became a semiprivate facility. The goal of the new owners was to make eighteen holes by converting four of the existing holes to

	1	2	3	4	5	6	7	8	9
Back	408	197	357	442	173	546	350	423	130
Middle	393	179	342	425	146	535	332	393	125
Men's Handicap	5	11	8	4	12	1	10	7	13
Par	4	3	4	4	3	5	4	4	3

	10	11	12	13	TOTAL
Back	498	427	459	400	4810
Middle	455	401	448	383	4557
Men's Hcp	2	6	3	9	
Par	5	4	5	4	52

3 HOLE	1	2	3	4	5	6	7	8	9
Front	315	132	294	345	99	460	270	318	92
Women's Handicap	5	11	8	4	12	1	10	7	13

13 HOLE	10	11	12	13	TOTAL	FRONT	TOTAL
Front	401	325	394	308	3445		
Women's Hcp	2	6	3	9			

A scorecard from the thirteen-hole Jefferson Golf Course. (*Jefferson Golf Course*)

house lots, retaining the remaining five holes, and constructing thirteen new holes on additional land the company had purchased.

All was going as planned until 2007, when the project failed financially. For three years the layout was fallow until a local businessman bought the land where new holes sit but did not have the capital to purchase the other five. They remain unused.

Jefferson GC is a nonprofit run by a charitable golf foundation. It has embraced its unique status, and the scorecards tout, "Where par is a whole new number."

That isn't in reference to just the thirteen holes; golfers can play loops of four, nine, thirteen, and eighteen holes.

Gilroy (Ca.) Golf Course also wants golfers to know something is different about its layout, so it is billed as "The 11-Hole Gem."

"We do try and capitalize on the fact we are a little unique," said Don DeLorenzo, the head golf professional, general manager, and operator of the layout.

While Gilroy has eleven holes, it has only ten greens.

"It's a neat little wrinkle," DeLorenzo said.

The first time through, the golfer plays holes one to nine. The second time around, the first six holes remain the same. Golfers then go to a completely different seventh hole. The eighth green is the same as the eighth green on the first loop, but the second time around the eighth tees are radically different. What that means is that it is possible to have two groups on the eighth hole at the same time, teeing off from different locations but ending at the same green.

DeLorenzo said it is an easily workable scenario as long as everyone stays in his or her assigned spots.

"I won't say we haven't had any altercations," DeLorenzo offered, chuckling. "There have been no murders."

The seventh hole is either 395 or 352 yards. Number eight plays 248 yards the first time and 338 the second.

Gilroy was founded as a nine-hole golf course in 1922. According to DeLorenzo, farmers and businessmen from the area built the layout mostly on land donated by a local family. Some of the course is on city waterworks property. For reasons unknown, in the early 1960s the alternate seventh hole was added.

Then in the 1970s, a par-3 was eliminated for safety reasons and another added later in the routing to take its place. Recently, the original green was uncovered and trees near it removed in an effort to "resurrect the hole," DeLorenzo said, moving Gilroy closer to being an eighteen-hole course.

"We're getting there one hole at a time," he said, laughing.

While that may not be a realistic goal, Gilroy might soon be "The 12-hole Gem."

For many years, the town of Worthington was a summer destination for the wealthy, who enjoyed the Berkshire Mountains and quiet of Western Massachusetts over the ocean getaways that many of their contemporaries preferred.

It was in 1904 that golf arrived in the way of a three-hole layout that was soon expanded to nine holes, and **Worthington Golf Club** was born. Some of the original tees are still visible.

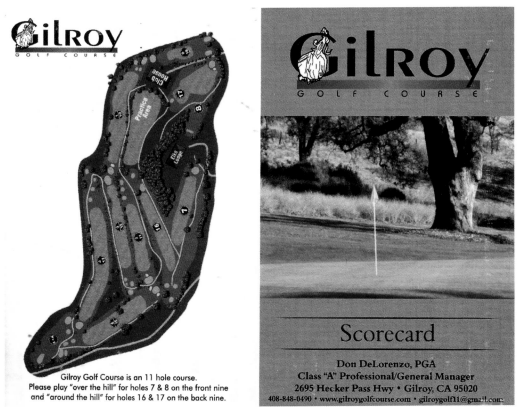

Gilroy Golf Course is an 11 hole course.
Please play "over the hill" for holes 7 & 8 on the front nine
and "around the hill" for holes 16 & 17 on the back nine.

Scorecard

Don DeLorenzo, PGA
Class "A" Professional/General Manager
2695 Hecker Pass Hwy • Gilroy, CA 95020
408-848-0490 • www.gilroygolfcourse.com • gilroygolf11@gmail.com

The layout from the Gilroy Golf Course showing the club's unique eleven-hole design. (*Gilroy Golf Course*)

For over a half century the configuration remained until the late 1970s, when the club's ambitious superintendent, Peter Bacon, came up with the idea of converting the small, inadequate driving range to a 10th hole.

Bacon was the first actual trained superintendent to hold the position at Worthington. His predecessors, according to longtime former member Steve Magaral, included "the farmer down the street."

Magaral said he was one of only a few members who practiced on the old range.

"I'd walk down there with a shag bag and whack a few 7-irons," he said.

He must have learned something while there. Magaral went on to attend Rollins College on a golf scholarship.

The concept for the addition moved forward thanks to a progressive executive board.

The membership liked the idea, and Worthington officially became a ten-hole layout, with the new hole a par-3 of approximately 170 yards.

It is played as the fifteenth hole for golfers going around two times. Worthington hosts an annual twenty-hole event in which the tenth hole is played twice.

Worthington counts George Schultz, Secretary of State under Ronald Reagan, as a member. Schultz grew up in nearby Cummington, where his father served as a selectman.

Acknowledgments

There are few absolute truisms in life. One of them, however, is that if you write a book you will inadvertently fail to acknowledge people who deserve the recognition. Whoever you are, I sincerely and wholeheartedly apologize.

I'd like to first thank John Sabino, who brought me into this wonderful project.

Thanks also to the good people at Skyhorse Publishing, especially my editor, Julie Ganz, for her infinite patience, wise counsel, and deft editing.

In no particular order, thank you to Ian Andrew, Jim Urbina, David Cage, Joel Larson, and Twin Pine Casino for the hospitality. Also to Marg and Brian McCann, Dick Silva, Curt Angell, Justin Gabrenas, Tony Mayfield, Michael Vessely, James Henderson, Chris Monti, Bobby Weed, PB Dye, Mark Hess, David Polk, Mike Hulbert, Michael Keiser, John Bradley, Michael Hughes, Matt Griffith, Michael Kelly, Ron Pfaefflin. Larry Hannafin, Stanley Thompson Society, John D. Smith, Jeff Mingay, Jamie Harris, Richard Hogarth, Pat McKinley, Don Skacan, and Svenerik Nilsen; and to Danielle Tucker for going above and beyond to get me Kahuku photos. To Marc Rolfing, Dan Hatfield, Rob Collins, Tad King, Patrick Boyd, Parker Oliver, Bill Power, John Mallon, Troy Sigvaldason, Patrick Law, Cary Collins, Susan Chapski, Jon Zolkowski Gaylord Schaap, Ed Bale, Ted Tom, Riley Johns, Keith Rhebb, Gregg Pascale, Anthony Buttvick, Bryan Moran, Chris Girling; my editor at *Superintendent* magazine, David Frabotta; Ivan Morris, Southbridge High School Class of 1981, especially Paul St. Pierre for his auto racing knowledge (Okay, now will you guys buy the book?), Geoffrey Childs, Tom Fagerli, Blake's Restaurant (Candor, N.C.); Buster's Southern Barbeque (Calistoga, Ca.); Broom's Bloom Dairy (Bel Air, Md.) and The Coop (Winter Park, Fla.).

Musical accompaniment provided by Elvis Johnson, drums; Bumpy Chimes, guitars; and Rick White, bass.

Bubba Gollareny in no way, shape, or form contributed to this book, no matter what he says.

Also thanks to Aaron Donnelli, Sean Tully, Jim Kennedy, Bret Lawrence, Brett Zimmerman, EJ Altobello for his wonderful photography and, along with Dave Steffen and Richard Bray, for improving my golf swing. Thanks to Maura Healey for standing up for what is right, and of course to Anne Guthrie.

Most special thanks to Michelle Johnson, DVM, for her diligence in researching Beyond the Green, for her patience in listening to my endless rambling about nine-hole minutiae, and for accompanying me on excursions to some of the finest nines, but most of all for finding the greenside bunker on the fourth hole at the long-lost Norfolk Downs.